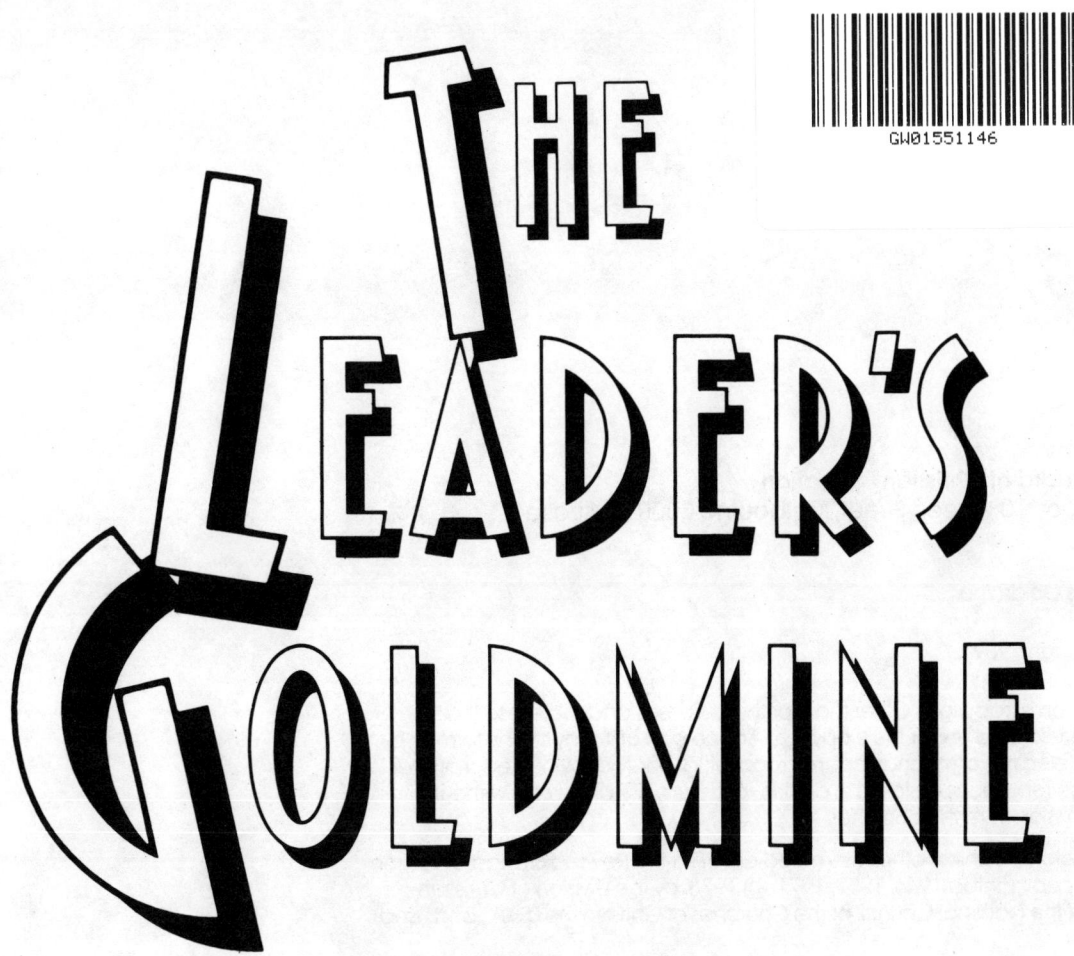

THE LEADER'S GOLDMINE

**Hundreds of ideas
for Christian groups**

Compiled by

Geoff Waugh

The Joint Board of Christian Education
Melbourne

Also by Geoff Waugh:
  Living in the Spirit (JBCE)
  Gifts of the Spirit (Serendipity)
  Fruit of the Spirit (Serendipity)

Published by
The Joint Board of Christian Education
Second Floor, 10 Queen Street, Melbourne 3000, Australia

The Leader's Goldmine

Scripture quotations unless otherwise noted are from the Revised Standard Version of the Bible, copyrighted 1946, 1952, 1971, © 1973, by the Division of Christian Education of the National Council of the Churches of Christ in the U.S.A., and used by permission.

Grateful acknowledgment is made to Serendipity Christian Resources, Australia and New Zealand for permission to use any material based on or adapted from Serendipity Christian Resources, Australia and New Zealand.

The author and compiler expresses his thanks for ideas and support given by groups and students he has worked with in developing this material.

National Library of Australia
Cataloguing-in-Publication entry
Waugh, Geoff.
The Leader's Goldmine: hundreds of ideas for Christian groups.
ISBN 0 85819 774 X.
1. Groups relations training — Religious aspects — Christianity. 2. Interpersonal relations — Religious aspects — Christianity. 3. Interpersonal communication — Religious aspects — Christianity. 4. Christian life. I. Waugh, Geoff. II. Joint Board of Christian Education.
248.4

First printed 1990

Cover design: Kelvin Young
Typeset: by Bookset Pty Ltd in Avant Garde
Printer: Shannon Press Pty Ltd   JB90/1789

Contents

How to use this book

The Leader's Goldmine gives you hundreds of ideas to use in any group. They aim to build relationship.

Choose the activities which interest you most. There is no set order, so use what appeals to you.

Ideas for building relationships are grouped in three categories called Deep, Deeper, and Deepest. The Deepest category needs a caring group willing to support and encourage one another.

Ideas for Bible studies and prayers encourage relational Bible study. They vary from specific comments on particular verses or topics to general suggestions on relational Bible study methods. Practical ideas about readings and prayers are included.

Ideas for church activities provide many suggestions for different groups in the church. Use the ones most suitable for your particular group.

Ideas for all ages together offer a wide range of activities you can use in various situations. They give you choices for family worship, intergenerational services, family camps, church family evenings, day camps and other times when all ages get together.

Ideas for integrated studies on themes give you a theme for a month. Each theme covers activites for personal, group, family and church use.

Group procedure
1. Relate in small groups of 4 to 5 people. More than 10 is difficult because large numbers mean less sharing for each person. Divide large groups into small sub-groups of 4 to 5, then everyone can speak and listen in relaxed comfort.

2. Allow up to half an hour for most of the activities. For example you may want to use one sharing activity and one Bible activity in an hour's session.

3. Meeting in homes, informally, is ideal — but anywhere will do. Home groups provide an excellent setting for relating together. Many of these activities can also be used with congregations such as in creative worship, family services, youth meetings or an informal evening service.

4. Be positive and encouraging. Avoid unkind comment. These activities can create an atmosphere of openness and acceptance. Then lives are changed. Fellowship and faith grow stronger.

5. Key words for vital group life are:
OPENNESS — as you open your lives to one another, love grows;
AFFIRMATION — as you support one another, faith grows;
ENCOURAGEMENT — as you enable growth in one another, hope grows.

Love one another
The Biblical basis for all these activities is the strong command to love one another. Many Bible passages emphasise that. Here are some:

love one another — John 13:34; 15:12, 17; Romans 12:10; 13:8; 1 Thessalonians 4:9; 1 Peter 1:22; 1 John 3:11, 23; 4:7, 11, 12; 2 John 1:5

serve one another — Galatians 5:13; 1 Peter 5:5

accept one another — Romans 15:7

strengthen one another — Romans 14:19

help one another — Hebrews 3:13; 10:24

encourage one another — Hebrews 10:25

forgive one another — Ephesians 4:32; Colossians 3:13

submit to one another — Ephesians 5:21

carry one another's burdens — Galatians 6:2

be tolerant with one another — Ephesians 4:2; Colossians 3:13

be concerned for one another — Hebrews 10:24

be kind and tenderhearted to one another — Ephesians 4:32

The relationship activities in this book give you plenty of scope to do all of that together.

To love one another does not mean becoming a cosy, self-centred clique. As Jesus demonstrated and taught, it means self-denial and sacrificial service for one another and for others. It involves close intimacy as well as deep involvement in the world's need or pain. Indeed, the more you are involved in serving God in the world, the more you need the close support of one another.

Jesus is our model. He shared his life deeply with Peter, James and John, and with the 12, as well as with others. Together they worked for the kingdom of God.

May God guide and bless your work. Successful mining!

Geoff Waugh

Ideas for building relationships

Deep — ideas and attitudes
Deeper — ideals and values
Deepest — ideologies and commitments

You can use these 200 Ideas for building relationships in many ways. Large groups could be divided into small groups of 4 or 5 people for relating together.

Some suggestions for activities 1-30 are:

a. Everyone in the group responds to an activity in turn. Discussion may follow.

b. One person responds to an activity leading into general discussion.

c. Each person selects an activity and responds to it.

For activities 30-200

d. Ask someone one of the questions. They respond and then they ask someone that question or another one.

e. One person in the group asks questions of each of the others. Then another person does the same.

f. Pick a number at random and respond to that question or task.

g. Write or type selected questions on paper or cards. Shuffle and take one in turn.

These activities can be used with all your friends, or any group, whether Christian or not. They may be a means of friendship evangelism as you share your ideas with one another.

Deep — ideas and attitudes

1. Activate encouragement Talk about the things that encourage people or groups. Encourage open sharing of ideas and attitudes.

2. Bible study Group Bible studies can be varied. See *Ideas for Bible studies and prayers*.

3. Buzz groups Discuss a question, topic or issue in small buzz groups of 4 or 5 people. Then report to the whole group.

4. Brief brainstorm Anyone can quickly give ideas on the topic. No discussion. Discuss it later on.

5. Case discussion Real or simulated situations and problems are presented for the group to suggest their solutions or decisions.

6. Circular response Allow everyone in turn to respond to a question, topic or issue without discussion. Discuss it after all have commented.

7. Controlled discussion People raise questions or comment but the discussion is controlled by the leader.

8. Counselling situation One person consults a counsellor or panel concerning a real or simulated situation or problem. Then the group may add their ideas.

9. Encounter group Group members discuss their relationships with each other to increase awareness and sensitivity.

10. Free-group discussion The group decides the topic and direction of discussion. Leaders, or later discussion, can reflect on what happened and why.

11. Group project Varied activities on a theme or topic usually organised into a presentation.

12. Group seminar Discussion introduced by the presentation of a paper, speech or other method which opens the topic.

13. Group tutorial A seminar directed by the leader or tutor.

14. Micro-teaching session Involvement in a learning situation which is observed then discussed.

15. Open education People choose their own goals and methods and work together with others who can help them achieve those goals. Leaders and resource people facilitate the process.

16. Paper collage Cut or tear pictures, headlines or articles from papers and magazines on a topic and discuss it.

17. Photographic sessions Planning, photographing and presenting results as a group task. Photos, slides, strip films, movies and videos can be used.

18. Project montage Create a 3-D expression on the topic using available materials.

19. Role play People participate by acting a role, spontaneous or prepared. This can also be done in discussion, e.g. discussing how the church can be more effective, with people taking roles such as a minister, elder, youth leader, parent, young person, politician, social worker, and so on.

20. Role reversal People can role play their opposite role or someone they differ from, e.g. parent/child, husband/wife, single/married, under 30/over 30, adult/youth, Christian/agnostic.

21. Recorded session Use audio or video tapes for personal interviews, group opinions, or the presentation of group responses to a topic or issue.

22. Practicum session The group participates in the learning process or task by attempting it.

23. Problem-centred groups Groups are given a specific task to discuss and report on or complete.

24. Simulation game A real situation is duplicated in its essential features. Leaders and later discussion reflect on what happened and why. See *Simulation activities and games*, page 35.

25. Step-by-step discussion The group follows a prepared sequence of questions or issues.

26. Symposium panel People represent different points of view on a topic. Each speaks in turn, then the whole group may interact.

27. Syndicate discussion Different small groups work on various aspects of a topic or issue and share their findings or insights with the whole group.

28. Synetics discussion A brainstorm in which people from diverse backgrounds or opinions contribute ideas to produce creative solutions.

29. Task groups Each group has a specific task such as answering a question, exploring a topic, completing a project, planning an event, or producing an item.

30. Topical issues Choose a topic of interest to you personally or to your group, and comment on it. This may lead into discussion. Lists like the following can be used to identify interests in your group, e.g. people write down or indicate the topics which interest them most.

Some examples:

advertising	leisure
alcohol	love and sex
communication	marriage
community needs	money
credit cards	mortgages
disease	news
divorce	nuclear arms
ecumenical movement	occult
education	politics
ethnic groups	race relations
faith	raising children
financial security	rock music
food	single parents
gambling	teenagers
gangs	travel
guns	unemployment
hunger	vandalism
inflation	war and peace
interest rates	violence
	others

Deeper — ideals and values

31. Activate strengths Talk about the strengths you see in each person in your group. Write down the comments you receive.

32. Avoiding things What things do you tend to avoid as long as you can?

33. Action replay What do you value most from your past?

34. Bedtime memory What is a happy childhood bedtime memory?

35. Childhood memory What is one of your special childhood memories?

36. Excitement and frustration What excites you most and frustrates you most about the topic? e.g. the church, TV, education, marriage, your family.

37. Family tradition What is a family tradition you value?

38. Fantasy holiday What holiday would you like most?

39. Fire drill What three things would you grab from your home if it burst into flames?

40. Free day If you could do anything on a free day, what would you do?

41. Friendship quality What is one quality you want in a friend? Why?

42. Fulfilling job What is one of the most fulfilling jobs you have ever had?

43. Future dreams Imagine yourself 5 or 10 years from now. What would you like to be doing? List some steps to help you fulfil that dream. Can the group help?

44. Goal setting Write down 3 major concerns or interests in your life. Choose one, and write a list of things you wish about it. Organise your wishes into a plan of action. The group may be able to add ideas to your list. You could use these headings:
a. my concerns
b. my wishes
c. my plans

45. Good time What is your idea of a good time? How does that affect your life?

46. Greatest success What do you see as one of your greatest successes in life? How does this affect your life now?

47. Group feelings How do you feel in a
a. large group?
b. small group?
c. discussion group?
d. sharing group?

48. Group goals What goals do you have as a group?

49. Group hopes What do you hope to get from your group experience and what would you like to give to the group?

50. Helpful advice What kind of advice do you find helpful?

51. Heroes analysis Who were your heroes or models in
a. primary school?
b. secondary school?
c. life after school?

52. Ignoring rules What are some rules you have ignored or would like to change?

53. Impossible dream Dream your impossible dream

about the ideal you have for your topic, e.g. our church, community, youth, old people. What can you do to move toward that ideal?

54. Improve life What would you like to do to improve the quality of life today?

55. Impulse buying What kind of things do you tend to buy on impulse?

56. Influential person Who has had the greatest influence in shaping your present thinking and attitudes? How did this happen?

57. Island adventure If you could have a year on an island, what would you take with you?

58. Life motto What motto would describe your attitude to life? Comment on the implications of the motto.

59. Magic box If you could get anything you wish from a magic box, what would you take
a. for yourself?
b. for someone else?
c. for each member in the group?

60. Major concerns What are 2 or 3 major concerns in your life just now and how can your group help you face, resolve or make the most of them?

61. One year If you knew you had one year left to live, what would you want to accomplish? Can the group help?

62. Peer pressure How does peer pressure affect you?

63. Personal achievement What is a personal achievement you are pleased about?

64. Personal ambition What is an important personal ambition you have?

65. Pin-up person Whom do you most admire? Why?

66. Present abilities What are 2 things you are good at doing? What can others in your group see that you are good at doing?

67. Present goals What are your goals in life at present? Can the group help toward fulfilling them?

68. Priority order Arrange a list of words in order of priority for you. Some groups could try to reach consensus about the order. Examples: health, wealth, children, fame, security, satisfaction, faith.

69. Quo vadis? Where are you going in life?

70. Resisting conformity What is something you did or are doing to resist conformity and be yourself?

71. School days What are your happiest or most significant memories of school?

72. Secret desire What secret desire to be someone or something did you have as a child?

73. Significant books What are 2 or 3 significant books which have affected your life?

74. Significant films What films have significantly influenced you?

75. Significant people Write down the names of 5 or more significant people in your life. Beside each name list a few things that person would want you to value or what they would expect of you. What have you learned?

76. Spontaneous action What is a spontaneous action you made and how do you feel about it?

77. Still searching What are you still searching for at this stage in your life?

78. Ten years Imagine yourself 10 years from now. What do you anticipate? You could note your ideas under these headings:
   a. goals now,
   b. 10 year goals,
   c. lifetime goals.

79. Think again What 2 or 3 things do you think about over and over again? How can that affect your living or attitudes.

80. Time again If you had your time over again, what would you like to change? How can this insight affect your planning or choices now?

81. Top priorities Describe your top priorities in life at present. Are you satisfied with these priorities?

82. Twenty pleasures List 20 things you love to do. Tick your top 5 preferences. Beside the full list indicate:
   $ — for those that cost money,
   A — for those you prefer to do alone,
   B — for those you would like to do better,
   C— for those which are conventional in your group.
What have you learned?

83. Unpleasant job What has been one of your most unpleasant jobs?

84. Urging telegram Write a 20 to 25 word telegram beginnng with 'I urge'. It may be for anyone living or in history and can indicate something you would like them to do.

85. Vacation plans Think of a vacation you could take that would really help in every area of your life. What would you do?

86. Wild adventure If you could embark on any wild adventure, what would you choose?

87. Word sequence Arrange a list of words in a sequence most meaningful to you. Examples: forgiveness, repentance, love, reconciliation, service.

88. Your comment Comment briefly on one, some or all the following:
   arriving late
   competition
   friendship
   habits
   healing
   honesty
   loneliness
   politics
   religion
   sex
   terminal illness

89. Your favourites Comment on your favourite (of one, some or all the following):

Bible passage	meal
book	movie star
car	music
character — fictitious,	party
historical	pet
dance	possession
film	song
food	sport
hobby	subject
job	time of day
leader	TV program
magazine	other favourites

90. Your ideal Comment on your ideal (one, some or all the following):

church building	outing
church community	party
church service	weekend
home	vacation
house	other
job	

Deepest — ideologies and commitments

91. Activate love The group expresses love to each member of the group in specific ways, e.g. gratitude, encouragement, prayer support.

92. Appreciate most What do you appreciate most about your
   a. family?
   b. friends?

93. Apprenticeship choice Write down the name of someone you would like to serve an apprenticeship with for a year. Add your reasons. Add the things you think you would be doing. As you discuss this, note ways some of these things may happen.

94. Autobiography summary Each person gives a brief autobiography of his or her life story. The group may respond with questions.

95. Being happy What makes you really happy, and what can people do to increase your happiness?

96. Being responsible What does being responsible mean for you?

97. Best quality What is the best quality you have?

98. Bottleneck blockage What are some bottlenecks in your life which seem to get in the way of other things you want to do? What can you do about these?

99. Biographical summary Each person writes a brief biographical summary of their life. These are read to the group by someone else and the group tries to identify the person from that summary.

100. Bible motto What statement from the Bible is a motto for you?

101. Big splurge If you could splurge to the limit of your possible credit, what would you do?

102. Change direction If you change your direction or yourself, what change would you like? Can the group help?

103. Changing circumstances How does your faith or beliefs adapt to changing circumstances?

104. Childhood embarrassment What is something that embarrassed you in childhood that you can laugh about now?

105. Childhood fantasy What fantasy from your childhood do you still hold or see being fulfilled?

106. Childhood fun What was your favourite fun activity as a child?

107. Childhood success What is something you achieved successfully in your childhood which pleases you?

108. Childhood table Draw a table top representing your childhood meal table. Select a colour for each person at the table and other significant people in your life then. Colour the table as you felt then. Comment on these relationships and feelings.

109. Close together What brings you close together with your
   a. family?
   b. friends?

110. Close to God What brings you close to God? What ideas does the group have?

111. Clothing styles What does your clothing say about you? Examples: casual, relaxed, colourful, modern, enduring.

112. Compliment received What is a compliment you received that you value?

113. Conversational prayer Pray together as in a conversation, allowing ideas to flow on naturally.

114. Creative art Express your feelings or attitude in creative art using pencil, biro, crayon, paint, etc.

115. Creative movement Express your feelings or attitude in movement such as dance, pose or mime.

116. Creative sculpture Express your feelings or attitude in sculpture using Plasticine, play dough, clay, your body, etc.

117. Creative writing Express your feelings or attitude in written form such as poetry, jingle, prose, song.

118. Crisis times What do you tend to do in a crisis?

119. Describing you Write down 3 words that each of these people might use in describing you: parents, teachers, friends, boy/girlfriend or spouse, yourself, people in your group. Check it out.

120. Descriptive verbs What three positive verbs ending in -ing describe you best? Others may like to add more.

121. Diary notes Make diary notes about 3 to 5 significant events in your life, what happened and how you feel about it.

122. Discovering yourself What experience helped you most to discover your potential, abilities or personality more fully? What did you learn about yourself?

123. Essential needs What are some needs which you regard as essential to your life?

124. Evaluation sheet Occasionally evaluate your group experience in writing answering such questions as:
   a. What was most helpful?
   b. What was least helpful?
   c. What would you like to do more often?

125. Experience more What do you wish you could experience more of:
   a. in your family?
   b. with your friends?

126. Extra ordinary What is something extra ordinary you would like to do or be involved in?

127. Family ritual What is a family ritual significant to you?

128. Family values Write in a column the things your family likes to do or values. Add these symbols to your list:
   o — for what brings you close together,
   I — for what brings you close to God,
   − — for what brings you close to other people,
   * — for what you really like to do.

129. Feel deeply What is something you feel deeply about? Why?

130. Feeling good What are you feeling good about in life just now?

131. Feelings doodle Doodle on blank paper to express your present feelings about a topic, e.g. yourself, home, the church.

132. Feelings wheel Draw a circle, divide it into quarters and in each quarter write one word which expresses how you feel here and now. Reflect on the balance in your here-and-now wheel.

133. Great expectations What are some of your great expectations in life?

134. Great experiences What are some great experiences you remember?

135. Greatest gift What is the greatest gift you can give to your:
    a. family?
    b. friends?

136. Greeting line Form two facing lines and greet the person opposite you in an appropriate way. Move left and greet the next person in line. Continue through the group. In discussion, reflect on the process.

137. Group journal Keep a journal in which you occasionally note significant insights gained from your group. Share these with the group at mutually agreed times.

138. Hand print Outline your hand on a blank sheet of paper. Write your name in the palm and these significant things on each finger:
    thumb — something you believe in strongly,
    index finger — something you are going to do,
    middle finger — something important to you,
    ring finger — someone important to you,
    little finger — something small but important.

You can discuss these in your small group or put them on the wall for the group to see.

139. Happiest week What was the happiest week you have lived? Reflect on the significance of that.

140. Happy Christmas What was a really happy Christmas for you?

141. Helping you How can people really help you,
    a. in your family?
    b. in your group?

142. Hot seat Volunteers, or all group members, are asked questions by the group for 5 to 10 minutes each. No discussion. The person in the hot seat may pass on any question.

143. House building The group can describe or build an imaginary house for each peson in the group. It can fit their personality, e.g. large windows (aware), rumpus room (enjoys fun), bright colours (sunny disposition).

144. Human warmth Where was the centre of human warmth in your childhood home and what security was associated with that?

145. Imagination meditation Close your eyes and imagine yourself in a beautiful scene. Then invite Jesus into it and allow him to direct your thoughts.

146. Important choice What was one of the most important choices you have made apart from becoming a Christian or choosing a spouse?

147. Influential experience What experience in life has had the greatest influence in shaping your present thinking and attitudes? How did it happen?

148. Introduce partners Talk for 5 minutes in pairs about yourself, what you have done and what you like. Then each person introduces their partner to the group noting some of their achievements and likes.

149. Life line Draw a line representing your life span. Above it indicate major periods in your life and below it write where you lived then. Draw symbols on the line representing significant events in your life.

150. Lifelong commitments What are some commitments you have made for life?

151. Like you What person is most like you, and in what ways? This may be from the Bible, history, fiction, TV, or people living today.

152. Making mistakes How do you handle making mistakes?

153. Mod cons If you had to do without some modern conveniences, what would you give up?

154. Most admired Who is someone outside your family you admire most?

155. Mountain peak Describe a mountain peak experience in your life or spiritual growth. What benefits continue from it?

156. Musical instrument What musical instrument are you like and why? Examples: solid base drum, soft harp, support strings.

157. Name chain Each person says their name and something they like. One person in the group starts by saying 'I am _____ and I like _____.' The next adds, 'He/she is _____ and he/she likes _____. I am _____ and I like _____.' Each person lists all the names and likes given so far and adds their own.

158. Newspaper report Duplicate or photocopy on sheets of paper some newspaper sections, e.g. headline, lead story, editorial, quote, letters to the editor, personal column, public notices, lost and found, avertisement, entertainment, financial, cartoon, comic strip, sport, weather, etc. Each person writes their name on their sheet and passes it clockwise round the group. Others add positive and affirming comments in the various sections.

159. Obituary tribute What are some comments you would like included in an obituary tribute to you?

160. Object study Choose an object from a collection of objects such as stones, apples, flowers, driftwood. It can represent you in some way.

161. Personal abilities What are 3 things you are good at doing and enjoy doing?

162. Personal commitment What are you personally committed to now?

163. Personal crest Draw or describe a personal crest which would indicate your values or goals in life.

164. Personal growth What are areas of personal growth for you and how do your strengths help that?

165. Personal habits What personal habits do you value or wish to adopt?

166. Personal history What have been the interesting and significant events in your personal history and how do those events shape your life now?

167. Personal motto What motto summarises your life?

168. Personal need Share a personal need with the group and then support one another, e.g. in prayer, action.

169. Personal poem Write a poem about your attitudes or values. Free verse is fine. Read and comment on it in the group.

170. Personal reference Write a reference of one paragraph about yourself which you regard as realistic and positive. Read it to your group. Others may like to add a sentence or phrase.

171. Personal satisfaction What brings you the greatest personal satisfaction? How could the group help you find this satisfaction more often?

172. Personal strengths What do you see as your greatest personal strengths? The group may want to comment on other strengths also.

173. Positive words What are 2 positive words you would like people to use in describing you after you are dead?

174. Prayer diary Keep a prayer diary and comment on it at your weekly group session. This can be personal comment, or group comment on your group prayer diary.

175. Primitive art Depict something about yourself, such as relationships, goals, dreams, in primitive art. Symbolism may be used.

176. Privacy circles Draw 5 concentric circles representing your widening contacts with people from (1) self, to (2) intimates, (3) friends, (4) acquaintances, and (5) strangers. Note in each circle things you could comfortably discuss there but not further out.

177. Reflective listening Listen to one person tell about their attitudes or feelings and then the group reflects back the feelings they hear, e.g. You feel pleased/frustrated/excited about . . .

178. Significant person Who is or was a significant person in your life outside your family?

179. Significant thing What significant thing has happened to you? This may be a funny thing, a happy thing, a serious thing, a silly thing, a stupid thing; or each of these.

180. Soul friend What would you look for in a soul friend?

181. Spiritual graph Draw a graph representing your spiritual journey. Use symbols to indicate significant events.

182. Strong value What is a particularly strong value you hold?

183. Success achieved What success have you achieved which really pleases you?

184. Symbolic gifts Give each person in your small group a symbolic gift suited to them, e.g. green light to go for it, compass for clear direction, log fire for warmth.

185. Taboo subjects What were some taboo subjects in your youth which you can talk about now?

186. Touched deeply What touches you most or really touches you deeply?

187. Touching you What film or book has touched you deeply?

188. Trust walk In pairs, one person leads a blindfolded partner by the hand on a trust walk. Then exchange roles. Reflect on your feelings and discoveries.

189. Turning point What was a major turning point in your life?

190. Understanding yourself Who has helped you to understand yourself the most? What did you learn about yourself?

191. Unique qualities What are some of your unique qualities?

192. Water description Describe your present state in terms of water, e.g. tumbling waterfall, soft mist, widening stream.

193. Weather description Describe your present state in terms of the weather, e.g. sunny, stormy, light rain, windy.

194. Week's review Review the high and low points of the past week. This can be a regular group activity.

195. When hassled What do you usually do when you are hassled?

196. White lie Would you ever tell a white lie? Comment.

197. Who's who? Write brief notes about yourself. Hand these to one person who reads them out and the group tries to identify each person from their description.

198. Who's you? The whole group responds to each question before moving on to the next one:
   a. Who are you?
   b. Who do you pretend to be?
   c. Who do you really want to be?

199. Written support Give the group blank paper. Everyone writes their name on the top and passes it clockwise for all the others to write affirming or appreciative comments on it. This can also be done on sheets of paper taped to people's backs or to painted walls with masking tape.

200. Your feelings When do you feel, or have felt (choose one, some, or all)

adventurous	hurt
angry	insecure
awkward	satisfied
confident	secure
excited	silly
frightened	peaceful
good	proud
happy	other

See also 60 questions in the *Family and church family questionnaires* on page 33 in the section on *Ideas for all ages together*.

Ideas for Bible studies and prayers

Bible passages
Bible study methods
Bible reading and relationship building
Bible readings and prayers

Bible passages

You can use these activities for any small group, or for a large group where you move into small clusters for about 15 minutes. They make ideal sharing activities for a group after brief comment about the passage. This collection of 50 relational Bible studies can provide weekly group devotions for a year. Use them in any order.

1. Activate prayer 1 Thessalonians 5:17, etc. — Share needs together and pray for one another.

2. Express prayer Philippians 4:6 etc. — Write 5 to 10 words which express how you really feel now, or which express your deep desires, longings or hopes. Then write a prayer in free verse using one of these words in each line, beginning with a word for the first line that is especially meaningful to you.

3. Favourite passage John 3:16, etc. — What is a favourite Bible passage of yours and why?

4. Bible motto Philippians 2:11, etc. — What verse or phrase from the Bible would you choose as a motto?

5. Solomon's choice 2 Chronicles 1:7, 11-12 — If God gave you the same offer given to Solomon, what would you ask?

6. Your house 2 Kings 20:1 — If your life was compared with a house, which room would need a little cleaning to be set in order?

7. Offering gifts Matthew 2:11 — What gifts would you like to offer Jesus? Can those gifts be expressed in prayer or service?

8. Assassination attempts John 5:18; 7:1, 19 — In what ways was Jesus a threat to others? In what ways is he a threat to you?

Note the assassination attempts on his life by sword (Matthew 2:16), cliff (Luke 4:29), stones (John 8:59), and plot (Mark 14:1).

9. Jesus the rebel Luke 4:18-19 — If Jesus came back in person today, what do you think he would change, and why?

N.B.: outcasts: Mark 2:16-17; Matthew 9:9-13; Luke 5:27-32; rich man: Matthew 19:16-30; Mark 10:17-31; Luke 18:18-30; temple row: Mark 11:15-19; Luke 19:45-48; Matthew 21:12-17; John 2:13-22; commandments: Mark 12:28-34; Matthew 22:34-40; Luke 10:25-28; leaders: Mark 12:38-40; Matthew 23:1-36; Luke 20:45-47.

You could divide a large group into 5 small groups, each one discussing one of these examples and then reporting back.

10. Your storm Mark 4:35-41 — Using the stilling of the storm as a parable or analogy of a stormy experience in your life, describe how you felt during the storm and how peace came to you. This could lead to group prayer.

11. Mary and Martha Luke 10:38-42; John 12:1-3 — Are you most like Mary or Martha?

12. Jesus wrote John 8:1-11 — What do you think Jesus may have written in the dust? Why?

13. Set free John 8:31-32, 36 — How do you understand being set free, and what degree of freedom do you think you have now? How could the truth available in your group help to free you more fully?

14. Beatitudes Matthew 5:3-10 — Which of the beatitudes are strongest in your life at present? You could rank yourself on each one from 5 (strong) to 1 (weak).

15. Salt Matthew 5:13 — In what ways are you like salt in (a) your home, and (b) your community, e.g. savouring, preserving, healing. What do you think Jesus is saying to you about being salt?

16. Light Matthew 5:14-16; John 8:12, 1 John 1:5 — In what ways do you show or reflect God's light? In what ways do you see that light in others in your group?

17. The Vine John 15:1-5 — What spiritual resources do you draw from the Lord? What helps you to draw on the life of the Vine? What hinders you from drawing on more spiritual resource?

18. Abundant life John 10:10 — What does abundant life mean for you?

19. The church Matthew 16:18 — What does the word church mean for you?

20. The body Romans 12:4-5; 1 Corinthians 12:12-27 — Using the analogy of the body, where do you feel you fit in, or what organ or member of the body depicts your function, e.g. ear, hand, heart, feet, etc.?

21. Your ministry Romans 12:6-8 — What do you see as your main ministry? What ministries do you see in others in your group?

22. Sport 1 Corinthians 9:24-27; Hebrews 12:1-2 — With the sports arena as a spiritual analogy, where would you place yourself at present — outside the grounds, in the grandstand, getting dressed, warming up, beginning, in full contest, winning, etc.? What weights hold you back? What is your immediate goal? What is your ultimate goal in life? How can the group help you achieve these goals?

23. Love 1 Corinthians 13:4-8 — Describe love in your own words.

24. Tug-of-war Galatians 5:17 — Where do you experience the greatest tug-of-war in your life? How can your group help you do what you want to do?

25. Fruit Galatians 5:22-23 — What does the word fruit mean for you in the fruit of the Spirit? What fruit is ripest in your life just now? How can the fruit ripen more fully in you?

26. Gifts of grace Ephesians 4:7 — What are the gifts of God's grace you see in people in your group, including yourself?

27. Being thankful 1 Thessalonians 5:16 — What are you really thankful about?

28. Practical commands 1 Thessalonians 5:14-22 — Which command do you find easiest to obey? Which command do you find most difficult to carry out? If you took the passage seriously, what difference would it make? Can the group help?

Other examples: Romans 12:9-21
Matthew 5 to 7 (selections)
Exodus 20:1-17

29. Encouragement Hebrews 10:24-25 — What can people do to encourage you?

30. Bible character you admire Hebrews 11:1-2 — Which Bible character, apart from Jesus, do you admire most, and why?

31. Bible character like you Hebrews 11:32 — Which Bible character is most like you, and why?

32. Bible characters in your group Hebrews 11:32, etc. — Which Bible characters are like the various people in your group? This can be generally talked about; or you can take each person in turn and indicate for them; or each person could write down the names of everyone in your group and the Bible character like them.

33. Bible history Hebrews 12:1 — Select figures in Bible history and list positive ways that you are like these people, and ways in which others in your group are like them. You could use some of the following names, and many others.

34. Adam and Eve Genesis 3:8 — In what ways and when do you try to hide from God?

35. Enoch Genesis 5:24; Hebrews 11:5 — In what ways have you walked with God?

36. Noah Genesis 6:14; Hebrews 11:7 — What impossible dream have you persevered with in your spiritual life?

37. Abraham Genesis 12:1 — What securities have you left behind to step out in faith, e.g. inadequate concepts of God, superstition, money?

38. Israel Genesis 32:28 — Jacob (the deceiver) was called Israel (prince with God). What encouraging name or title would you give to each person in your group, including yourself?

39. Joseph Genesis 45:7-8 — When has God worked in your circumstances to bless you and others?

40. Moses Exodus 3:11, 13; 14:1, 10, 13 — When have you agrued with God?

41. David Psalm 51 — When has a crisis in your life led to new blessing?

42. Mary Luke 1:48 — In what ways has God surprised and blessed you?

43. Jesus' life John 1:14 — What impresses you most about Jesus' life?

44. Jesus' death Mark 10:45 — What impresses you most about Jesus' death?

45. Jesus' resurrection and glory Matthew 28:18 — What impresses you most about the risen Jesus?

46. Peter Matthew 14:29 — When have you stepped out for God in new ways?

47. Stephen Acts 7:54-60 — When has it cost you something or required courage for you to serve God or witness?

48. Paul Acts 9:4-6; 1 Corinthians 15:8-10 — In what ways has God changed you?

49. Hallelujah Revelation 19:1 — Express the word Hallelujah in any way that is meaningful to you, e.g. drawing or painting, writing a prayer or poem or letter, singing.

50. Compose your own Here are questions you can use with any passage:
a. Ask any or all of these:
What impresses you most about this verse or passage?
What inspires, convicts, or challenges you in this verse or passage?
What is God saying to you through this verse or passage?
b. Discuss these 4 questions:
What was the word there and then?
What was the issue there and then?
What is the issue here and now?
What is the word here and now?

Bible study methods

These relational Bible study methods have been compiled and summarised from a wide range of sources. You can adapt them to suit your group's size and style. Select a method that best fits the Bible passage you want to study.

Depth and encounter (Ross Snyder)
1. Individual work (in silence)
a. Paraphrase. Re-write the passage in your own words, as *you* would say it. Keep roughly to the same length as the original.
b. Think about the passage. Ask yourself: If I took this passage seriously, how would I be different? What situation or persons would I view differently?

2. Small group work Each person shares his/her paraphrase and thinking with the small group. Avoid discussion at this stage. Discussion may follow after everyone has shared their work, if time permits.

3. Whole group work Anyone shares any point which impressed them most in the small group sharing. 'What was a compelling word of God from this study which moved you to some specific response?' Keep sharing brief. Conclude with general discussion or comment.

Scripture analysis study
(Billy Graham Association)
1. Discovery What does the passage say? Write the passage in your own words. Keep to 6-8 words per verse. How would it read in a newspaper?

2. Understanding
a. What don't I understand? Be honest.
b. What is the key verse? Why?

3. Application
a. What impresses me most? Write that out using the personal pronoun 'I'.
b. Where do I come short in this? Be specific.
c. What do I intend to do about it, with God's help? Write a specific response.

This personal study may also be used for small group sharing leading to prayer for one another.

Depth-sharing sessions
(Lyman Coleman, Serendipity Series)
1. Preliminary exercise *(15 minutes)*
a. Note one or more of these symbols beside each verse:
✓ if you understand the verse clearly
? if you have a question about the meaning
* if you get special inspiration from the verse
+ if you get really convicted about something in your life.
b. Re-write in your own words any two verses which speak to your need or situation. Be personal and practical.
c. Application: Write down a need in your life at the moment. Ask yourself, 'As far as these two verses are concerned, what is the thing I must work on in my life?'

2. Small group interaction *(30 minutes)* Share your paraphrases in groups of 4.

3. Depth encounter *(15 minutes)* Share application in the same groups of 4. Pray specifically for each other.

Iona method
1. READ the passage aloud to the group, by one or more persons.

2. MEDITATE on the passage individually for 5 to 10 minutes.

3. EXPRESS to the group thoughts that come to mind, preferably everyone sharing their response.

Swedish method
1. READ the passage aloud to the group.

2. THINK about the passage and study it individually for 10 minutes.

3. WRITE personal responses to the passage in three sections beside these symbols:

question mark: note words, expressions or verses which you question, either because you don't understand them or you don't agree with them.

arrow: note what challenges, pricks the conscience, or ever gets under the skin.

candle: note thoughts which take on a new clarity or throw light on the rest of the passage or on some personal needs or problems.

4. SHARE these responses individually and allow group discussion which does not develop into debate or argument. Emphasise the value of the passage for each person.

Head, heart and hand

1. HEAD Here the facts about the passage are discovered: the meaning of words, for what, to whom and by whom it was written.

2. HEART Each person tries to discover the heart of the passage for himself or herself. Share these thoughts with a small group.

3. HAND What action should be taken as a result of reading this passage? Action often falls into these categories:
   a. Some group action for church or community.
   b. Further study to understand the real issues.
   c. Individuals changing attitudes or behaviour.

Small groups could report to the total group about their responses.

Silence and sharing

1. ASK the group to look at the passage silently and choose the verse, phrase, word or thought which stands out most to each person.

2. SHARE these findings and the reasons why the verses or thoughts were chosen.

Eight questions

1. What are the scenes?

2. What are the difficult words?

3. What is the relationship of this passage to the context?

4. Why is it in the Bible at all?

5. What is the central meaning?

6. Can you illustrate this central truth from church history of the church today?

7. What is the meaning of the passage for our group and how does it affect the content of our life and faith today?

8. What act of obedience follows from this for the Christian community and what can my response be?

Depth Bible study

1. Read the passage, silently or aloud.

2. What did it mean when first written?

3. What does it mean for us today?

4. What does it mean to you?

5. Write a personal paraphrase and read it to the group.

Personal response

(written, then shared with the group)

1. I SEE .... observation of passage

2. I THINK .... opinion on passage

3. I FEEL (don't add 'that') ...... openness to passage

Inductive discovery study

1. SEE THE ISSUE What is the issue raised by this passage for us today?

2. ASSESS THE ISSUE What is involved for us in this issue and how does the passage help us?

3. ACT ON THE ISSUE What action is needed today to address the issue and how does the passage help us do that?

Meditation and prayer

1. READ the passage to the group slowly. Each person closes their eyes and imagines the scene then or applies it to their situation now.

2. MEDITATE individually on the scene or situation personally in silence for 3-5 minutes.

3. PRAY silently, responding to the Spirit's leading arising from the passage.

This study can lead to sharing in small groups and praying together about the concerns or responses raised by the study.

Bible reading and relationship building

These sessions may be used for relationship building using a Bible passage as a discussion starter. Work in groups of 4 or 5. Omit any session not relevant to your group.

1. Orientation
Devotional
What impresses you most about Jesus' character? (John 1:14)

Group work
What kind of person are you?
What influences helped to shape you?
Write down your earliest memory then note what that memory may say about your early life.
Pray, giving thanks for past blessings.

2. Personality development
Devotional
What can people do to encourage you? (Hebrews 10:24)

Group work
What characteristics have you inherited?
What two people had formative influence on you? Why?
Briefly describe your ideal man or woman. What do you learn about yourself from that?
What role in life do you find most satisfying? Why?
How do you personally decide what is right and wrong?
How would you summarise your world view or philosophy of life?
Pray, giving thanks for present growth.

3. Relationships
Devotional
Love is . . . (Mark 12:30-31)

Group work
What is one of your greatest personal successes or achievements?
What is one of your family's greatest successes or achievements?
What are 2 happiest events in your life?
Name 2 things you are good at doing.
State 3 words you would not like used about you.
State 3 words you would like used about you.
Name some strengths you see in each person in your group.
Pray, thanking God for your God-given strengths.

4. Marriage and family
Devotional
Are you like Mary or Martha, and how do you feel about the other? (Luke 10:38-42)

Group work
What do you want out of your marriage or family?
What strengths do you see in yourself, your spouse and/or your family to achieve this?
What changes are needed in yourself to achieve this?
If your family were everything you wanted it to be, how would you describe it in brief phrases?
What would you like your family to attempt or achieve before you part?
What has been one of your happiest family achievements?
Pray, including thanks and prayer for your family.

5. Children
Devotional
What childlike qualities do you admire in people? (Matthew 18:1-5)

Group work
What are some of your happiest childhood memories?
What memories about your children give you joy?
What do you enjoy doing with your children?
What do you find tough with your children?
What are some dreams you have for your children?
What can you do to help those dreams eventuate?
Pray, including thanks and prayer for your children.

6. Adolescence
Devotional
What is one of your faults or weak areas? (James 5:16)

Group work
What were 2 main problems you faced in adolescence and how did you handle them?
What were 2 main successes you had as a teenager?
Who were your heroes in your teens and how did they influence you?
What life-long commitments did you make as a teenager?
How do you think you can help adolescents today?
Pray, including thanks and prayer about teenage commitments.

7. Personal growth
a. STRUGGLE

Devotional
What motivates you to grow? (2 Peter 3:18)

Group work
What is an area of greatest present growth for you?
What is an area of struggle or difficulty?
What habits have you broken or changed?
What goals are you setting yourself?
What kind of weather would describe you now?
Pray, supporting one another in these areas.

b. STRESS

Devotional

What fruit of the Spirit do you have most and least? (Galatians 5:22-23)

Group work

What really makes you angry?
How do you handle anger?
What causes you most stress?
How have you handled strong urges to quit?
How did someone help you when you were struggling?
Pray, responding to needs in your group.

c. STRENGTHS

Devotional

What strengths and gifts do you have? (Romans 12:6-8)

Group work

What kind of person do you not want to be?
What kind of person do you want to be?
What growth do you see in yourself now?
What have you appreciated most about each other person in your group?
Give symbolic gifts to one another (e.g. a welcome mat, a telephone, a postage stamp — to stay in touch).
Pray for each person in your group in turn.

Bible readings and prayers

Neither Bible reading nor prayer need be boring. Both can be interesting. These suggestions will help you plan for meaningful Bible reading and prayer.

Bible readings

1. **Solo reading** — one person reads, well.

2. **Silent reading** — no voices used. This may lead into prayer or discussion: e.g. extempore prayer, or conversational prayer based on the passage read; discussion on the most significant thought read by each person, etc.

3. **Unison reading** — by the whole group.

4. **Choral reading** — by a small group to the whole group, in various ways.

5. **Choral speaking** — memorized by a small group and recited, in various ways.

6. **Dramatic reading** — direct speech ready by individuals; story by narrator.

7. **Dramatic speaking** — as above, but memorized.

8. **Alternate reading** — different voices reading alternately; e.g. leader and group, men and women, adults and children, two halves of a group.

9. **Responsive reading** — alternate reading where the second part responds to the first, e.g.
    A. The Lord is my Shepherd . . .
    B. Jesus said, 'I am the good shepherd . . .'
    A. He makes me lie down in green pastures . . .
    B. He shall feed his flock like a shepherd . . .
OR, Bible readings, with responses from hymns, etc.

10. **Antiphonal reading** — alternate readings where the second part echoes the first; e.g. as in Psalms or some prophetic passages, often divided at the colon, such as in Psalm 23, Isaiah 53.

11. **Litany reading** — another responsive reading where responses are identical, e.g. Psalm 136, or Psalm 107:1, 8, 15, 21, 31.

12. **Bible mosaic** — various verses are assembled to follow a theme, and may be presented in many different ways.

13. **Circular reading** — each person reads in turn around the circle, or room.

14. **Call reading** — each reader calls on someone else after reading the verse or section, and that other person continues the reading.

15. **Parallel readings** — various different translations of the verse(s) or passage(s) are used, and may be read in a variety of ways, e.g. different people reading different versions.

16. **Memorised readings** — the whole group (or a selected panel) participate by recalling verses, passages or phrases on a given theme, e.g. love.

17. **Bible drill** — the verse or passage in use (possibly a selection of verses) is called, and the first to locate it stands, then reads when others have also located the place. Useful for work with children; may be varied, e.g. the reading could be in unison, particularly for adults.

18. **Comparison readings** — where a passage is recorded in different books of the Bible these passages can be read (e.g. by different people) for comparison, e.g. similar passages in the Gospels, or in Kings and Chronicles.

19. **Chosen reading** — each person, preferably in small groups, chooses a reading. This may be on a given theme; or it may be significant verses, etc.

20. **Think and read** — people look at a given passage, think about it briefly and then read the verse, phrase or thought that impresses, challenges, helps, or disturbs them most.

Prayers

1. **Bible prayers** — read by an individual, the whole group, or different people reading different verses or sections, e.g. Matthew 6:9-13; Luke 11:2-4; 1 Chronicles 29:10-13; Psalm 51 (selections).

2. **Read prayers** — from books of prayers.

3. **Written prayers** — people in the group write their own prayers and then read them; or they may be written before the group meets.

4. **Silent prayer** — meditation.

5. **Guided meditation** — silent prayer with the aid of some guidance, e.g.
   a. musical background, using appropriate hymns;
   b. quiet reading, using appropriate Scripture, quotations;
   c. suggestions for prayer made by one person, or various people.

6. **Request and response** — one person (or various people) request prayer for or about specific areas (including praise, thanks and worship) and people respond in prayer as they desire.

7. **Bidding prayer** — leader bids worshippers to pray about things or people, and then waits while all pray silently, or in small groups; e.g. Let us give thanks for God's goodness during the past week.

8. **Prayer groups** — the whole group huddles into small prayer groups of 3 or 4 people, and prays together.

9. **Sentence prayers** — individuals pray aloud briefly. Some may want to pray more than once.

10. **Chain prayer** — each person prays in turn around the circle, or room. Written prayers, or read prayers may be used effectively this way also.

11. **Conversational prayer** — very effective, where people join in briefly to continue the thought or theme raised by the previous person, as in a conversation. Some people may join in many times.

12. **Extempore prayers** — individual prayers, not previously prepared.

13. **Unison prayer** — repeated together as a group, e.g. The Lord's Prayer; read prayers, etc.

14. **Hymn prayers** — sung, or spoken; individually or by the whole group, e.g. Abide with Me; Rock of Ages; Lead Kindly Light, etc.

15. **Litany prayers** — the group responds with identical prayers, e.g. If we have been unkind and hurtful, FORGIVE US, LORD, WE PRAY; If we have failed to obey you, FORGIVE US, LORD, WE PRAY or — LORD, HEAR OUR PRAYER.

16. **Responsive prayer** — the group responds with different prayers, e.g. to news items. These may be written by the group; read from prepared prayers, etc.

17. **Collect** — includes most aspects of prayer, and often used as introductory prayer. May be read individually, in unison, responsively.

18. **Choral prayer** — recited (or read) by a prepared group to lead in worship; may be spoken, or sung.

19. **Creative prayer** — expressed in some form of creative activity, e.g. poem, song, art (drawing, painting, design, etc.), dance or movement, sculpture (with Plasticine, play dough or modelling clay).

20. **Personal prayer** — often effective in small groups, where each person shares personal desires or needs about which the group can pray; or the group may pray for each other without any such prior sharing. This can be done in various ways, e.g. any person for anyone, pairs pray for each other, each prays for the person on their right (or right and left), each prays for all.

Ideas for church activities

Program emphases
Devotional
Educational
Creative
Serving
Social
Sporting
Witness and sharing weekend
Survey questionnaire
Commitment indicator
Interests indicator
Gifts check list

This collection of ideas and activities can be used in many different groups in a variety of ways.

You may reproduce the pages in this section for your own group use provided:

1. you make no charge for the reproduction

2. you acknowledge the source as *The Leader's Goldmine* by Geoff Waugh, © The Joint Board of Christian Education, 1990. Used with permission.

Program emphases

Use these ideas to enliven your programs,
and as a springboard to adding your own ideas.

Devotional

Bible quizzes: e.g. True/false, sentence completion, multiple choice, Who am I?, Bible Cricket (teams compete);

Worship centres: 3D, posters, symbols, montage, collage, assemblage, candles, etc.

Church service: Plan and present, worship-in-the-round, visit other churches, worship with music, drama, discussion, group participation;

Speakers: Visitors, challenge the Minister, missionary, church members;

Themes: Hymn analysis, it's Greek to me (on N.T. words), Bible people, map project (e.g. Paul), build a church (group's ideas);

Activities: Poster, prayers, mime and drama, pantomime, devil's advocate (e.g. why church is bad), casting lots (prayer ballot), including devotional use of all the following Program Ideas;

Relational studies: See *Ideas for Bible studies and prayers*.

Educational

With specialists: lecture, visiting speaker, interview, imaginary interviews, demonstrations, visits, field trips, Christian vocations, teach-in, electives, workshops, seminars, research;

With the group: discussion, questions, buzz groups, circular response, debate, impromptu group debate, panel, forum, case study, quotations, opinion polling, drama, play reading, open-ended drama, script writing, radio plays, tape recorded plays, verse drama, choral reading, mime, role plays, parent and child night;

With equipment: films, TV, cinema, filmstrips, slides, recordings, charts, maps, paintings, photographs, musical instruments, percussion, crazy otto (crazy orchestra, musical games), top ten hits (why?), magazines (evaluate, discuss), news headlines (of note for you), comics (Peanuts etc.), cassette library, record library.

Creative

Writing: poems, prayers, hymns, songs, plays, stories, captions and titles, group newspaper, monthly magazine, dictionary, letters;

Drawing and painting: (with pencil, craypas, crayons, texta colours, paint) brushes, finger painting, composite pictures, posters, murals, frieze, comic strip, potato designs, designs, symbolism, abstract, stick men, splatter painting, leaf prints, splodges, symmetrical art;

Modelling: Plasticine, clay, dough, play-doh, papier-mache, relief maps, sand;

Models: cardboard, paper, paper-folding, pipe cleaners, play board, materials;

Scenes: cut-outs, montage (paper pasted), collage (various textures), mosaic, assemblage (3D, from junk), diorama (with backdrop), panorama, flannelgraph, TV production, slide making, film making;

Dramatization: posing, mime, dramatic story, acting, scripted plays, writing and presenting plays, radio and tape recorded plays, TV plays, tableau, presenting for photographs/slides/filmstrips/films, free acting, street theatre, role playing, role reversal, verse, puppets (finger, stick, paper bag, hand, wooden spoon, shadow);

Music: listening — records, cassettes, live productions, TV producing — instruments, percussion, rhythmic movements, singing, inventing songs, dance, bands, orchestra, cassette.

Serving

Indoors:

house cleaning — for sick, elderly, single parents, working mothers

visiting — elderly, sick, prisoners (arranged with chaplains), hospitalised, retirement homes

singing groups — in visiting or arranging meetings, carols

use videos or films — with shut-ins, ill, elderly

soup kitchens — providing meals, snacks, entertainment

craft activites — at homes or in hall

offering short courses — e.g. T.A.F.E. on painting, drawing, writing, craft, community singing;

Outdoors:

lawn mowing — for sick, elderly, singles, working mothers

painting — fences, houses, windows, stairs

working bee — cleaning yards, gardening, removing rubbish

car wash — to raise money or voluntary

meals on wheels — to shut-ins, sick, elderly

shopping — for elderly, sick, needy

driving people places — outings, meetings, visiting

neighbourhood singing — carols, busking, park entertainment

street theatre — entertainment to raise money or voluntary

youth care team — meeting needs, outings, picnics

outings — picnics, day visits, day camps, excursions

door to door — offering help as a service.

Social

Indoors:

Indoor games (salamagundi or tabloid sports) — See Sporting, Creative social activity (as above), origami, soap carving, fancy dress, bring a friend, half and half (with another group), pet night, baby show, photograph gallery, everyone's birthday, elections, Celebrity Game, and I've Got a Secret (as on TV);

Outdoors, etc.:

Collecting for . . . (e.g. for needy), outings, barbecue, camp fire, progressive supper, window shopping, Scouts' week (finding and meeting community or personal needs, e.g. lawn mowing, gardening);

Organisational:

Involvement with community activity, e.g. social clubs, community projects, school activities, church projects, radio and TV communications, community resource centres.

Sporting

Without equipment:

indoor games — like poison spot, hit the deck, dog and bone, O'Grady (Simon says), Noughts and Crosses (with people);

outdoor games — like the above, and athletics, relays (file, exchange, in-and-out relay, circular) — with running, walking, hopping, crawling, sideways gallop, frog hops, kangaroo or rabbit jumping, backwards, skipping, Red Rover, Chinese wall, city gates, twos and threes, numbers, hoppo-bumpo, fox and geese, crusts and crumbs, rats and rabbits, hide and seek, chasings, swimming, water play, etc., hiking, walk rally, walk-a-thon, boat and bus trips;

With equipment:

indoor games — like table games, board games, musical games (e.g. over the broom, musical chairs, folk dances);

ball games — like relays (tunnel ball, overhead ball, circle gap, captain ball — file, line or circular), bouncing, throwing, dribbling, kicking — individually or in groups; bomb the centre, tower ball (centre man guards tower), golf, French cricket, circular or passing rounders, Countries;

team games — bowling, soft ball, volley ball, soccer, football, hockey, cricket, basketball, polo, water polo;

individual competitive games — tennis, table tennis, squash, golf, mini golf, shooting, and personal skills like skiing, water skiing, horse riding, bike riding, motor cycling, roller skating, ice skating.

Witness and sharing weekend

These suggestions are adapted from Lay Witness Mission materials prepared by Walter Albritton and Ben Campbell Johnson of the United Methodist Church in America and materials used for Lay Witness Missions in South Africa.

A local church can use these basic ideas for a special weekend of mission together. They are ideally suited to use with a visiting team of Lay Witness people who share their testimonies during the weekend and participate in groups with the local people.

The organizing team makes arrangements and meets during the weekend to monitor developments. Planning before, during and after the weekend could include task groups or committees for Prayer, Visitation, Home Groups, Transport, Publicity, Literature and Accommodation if visitors are involved.

This program can also be adapted for a weekend camp or retreat, such as a church family camp. The group questions for Saturday can then be divided into 3 for the morning and 3 for the afternoon.

Suggested program -- adapt as needed

Friday
5.30 p.m.	Visitors meet locals. Team meeting for final preparation.
6.30 p.m.	Congregational evening meal and fellowship.
7.30 p.m.	Worship and some testimonies.
8.30 p.m.	Small Groups
9.30 p.m.	Drinks available before leaving.

Saturday
7.30 a.m.	Prayer breakfast (optional)
8.30 a.m.	Team meeting, to reflect and plan together.
9.30 a.m.	Depart for home groups.
10.00 a.m.	Home Groups
1.00 p.m.	Luncheons for men and women, or in homes.
3.30 p.m.	Optional Groups.
5.30 p.m.	Team meeting.
6.30 p.m.	Congregational evening meal and fellowship.
7.30 p.m.	Worship and some testimonies.
8.30 p.m.	Small Groups
9.30 p.m.	Sanctuary open for prayer and meditation.

Sunday
7.30 a.m.	Breakfast in homes.
8.30 a.m.	Team meeting (depending on church service times).
9.30 a.m.	Worship service, or at normal time.
11.00 a.m.	(or earlier) Fellowship over drinks.
12 noon	Farewell luncheon if visitors are involved.
1.30 p.m.	Visitors depart (or earlier if not staying for lunch).
7.30 p.m.	Evaluation and projections by the church fellowship.

Group sessions

Friday night
1. What are you hoping will happen in the church as a result of this weekend?

2. What are you expecting for yourself?

3. What can we do as individuals to reach these goals?

Saturday
Quiet Time and Meditation followed by group sharing.
1. At what time in my life was God most real to me?

2. What is the most vivid experience of prayer that I have had?

3. If I had three wishes for all of life, what would I choose? Which of these would I choose above all others?

4. What is the most pressing need in my life?

5. How can I truly know God so that his presence is real and meaningful in my total life?

6. How may I effectively share with others what I have discovered about God?

Saturday night
1. Who is my audience? Before whom am I playing my life? Whose approval do I seek?

2. What are my specific points of resistance to the total will of God in my life?

3. Am I willing to give as much of myself as I can to as much of God as I understand — now?

4. What does total commitment mean for my life?

The Leader's Goldmine by Geoff Waugh, © The Joint Board of Christian Education, 1990. Used with permission.

Survey questionnaire

This survey questionnaire has been prepared by teams at the Gateway Baptist Church in Brisbane where it has been used in door to door visiting in pairs to identify community needs, make contact with people, and for friendship evangelism. You could use it or adapt it for your situation. Note that you need to follow up areas of need or interest if they are expressed.

Survey

Suburb _____ Date _____

'Hi/Hello, I'm _____ and this is _____.

We're from _____ and we're conducting a survey of community needs. Could I have a few minutes of your time so I can complete the survey?'

M ____ F ____ Approximate Age ____

1. What do you feel is the greatest community need in this area?
____ neighbourhood social activity
____ childrens playing areas
____ police security
____ special facilities
____ day care centres
____ public transport
____ other

2. What have you found to be the greatest pressure on family life in this community?
____ marital conflict
____ job satisfaction and conditions
____ child rearing
____ domestic security
____ loneliness
____ financial pressure
____ teenage parenting
____ other

3. What have you found to be the greatest personal needs of individuals in this community?
____ loneliness
____ spiritual well being
____ peace of mind
____ poor self image
____ lack of purpose or destiny
____ coping with stress
____ other

4. What advice would you give to a group that really wants to help people?

5. Do you belong to any religious group? Specify.

6. How often do you attend church?
____ weekly
____ monthly
____ once or twice a year
____ less often
____ never

7. Why do you think people in this community should attend church?

8. If you were looking for a church, what features would attract you?

9. How often do you pray to God?
____ daily
____ weekly
____ monthly
____ less often
____ only in grim situations
____ never

10. How often does God answer your prayers?
____ always
____ mostly
____ occasionally
____ I think he does
____ never

11. Do you believe you're going to heaven?
____ yes
____ no
____ unsure
____ don't believe in heaven or life after death

12. If God said to you 'Why should I allow you into my heaven?' what would you say?
____ unsure
____ other

Thank you for your time and interest. Would you like us to call back with the survey results?
____ yes
____ no
____ maybe

Name (if offered) _____

Address _____

_____

The Leader's Goldmine by Geoff Waugh, © The Joint Board of Christian Education, 1990. Used with permission.

Commitment indicator

This list can be circulated in your group or church for people to indicate what they are interested in or willing to do.

Important! If you use this, or adapt it, you must follow it through by giving people opportunity to talk about their interests and involvement.

My commitment
Please tick the ways in which you would like to be involved in church life in addition to your personal prayer and individual obedience to the Lord.

Church meetings
- ☐ Regular attendance at church services:
    - ☐ morning
    - ☐ evening
- ☐ Taking part in church services:
    - ☐ praying
    - ☐ reading
    - ☐ speaking
    - ☐ singing, or choir
    - ☐ playing an instrument
    - ☐ welcoming people
    - ☐ ushers
    - ☐ tidying
- ☐ Assisting in nursery
- ☐ Teaching Sunday School
- ☐ Involvement in a home group, prayer group, study group
- ☐ Providing hospitality for a home group
- ☐ Involvement in organisations for:
    - ☐ children
    - ☐ youth
    - ☐ women
    - ☐ men
    - ☐ adults
    - ☐ families
    - ☐ singles
    - ☐ recreation
- ☐ Attending training courses for:
    - ☐ Sunday School teaching
    - ☐ Youth work
    - ☐ Home group leadership
    - ☐ Counselling
    - ☐ Outreach
- ☐ Helping with baby-sitting
- ☐ Providing transport

Church maintenance
- ☐ Care of the property:
    - ☐ lawn mowing
    - ☐ gardening
    - ☐ painting
    - ☐ repairs
- ☐ Cleaning:
    - ☐ worship centre
    - ☐ church facilities
- ☐ Arranging flowers and greenery

Church extension
- ☐ Visiting:
    - ☐ the sick, old, lonely
    - ☐ church families
    - ☐ families interested in the church
    - ☐ people who may be interested
    - ☐ door to door
- ☐ Contacting people by telephone
- ☐ Telephone counselling (including training)
- ☐ Helping in letter-box distribution
- ☐ Distributing leaflets or magazines
- ☐ Helping in church library:
    - ☐ getting established
    - ☐ follow up loans
    - ☐ providing or lending books
    - ☐ providing or lending cassettes
- ☐ Helping in sale of books and cassettes
- ☐ Teaching Religious Education in schools
- ☐ Using your vocational skills, e.g. finance, media, repairs
- ☐ Secretarial help, e.g. typing, duplicating, mailing
- ☐ Preparing food for church functions
- ☐ Providing hospitality, e.g. visitors, boarders
- ☐ Volunteering for part-time or full-time church work
- ☐ Giving money
- ☐ Serving on committees or task groups
- ☐ Being a church member
- ☐ Any other activity or interest, e.g. sewing, signwriting

Name: ....

Address: ....

....

Telephone: ....

The Leader's Goldmine by Geoff Waugh, © The Joint Board of Christian Education, 1990. Used with permission.

Interests indicator

Discover the interests of your group. Use or adapt this list for people to indicate their interests.

Church directories or group directories can include the names, addresses, phone numbers, vocation and interests of each person. If used in a directory, the numbered list is usually given at the back of the directory and the numbers for each person's interests added after their name, address, vocation and phone number.

Your computer experts can run programs giving the names of all people interested in each topic and can regularly up-date your directory.

1	Aeromodelling	51	Cockatoos	101	Indoor Cricket
2	African Violets	52	Coins	102	Indoor Plants
3	Agricultural Shows	53	Compact Discs	103	Interior Decoration
4	Amateur Radio	54	Computers	104	Jazz Ballet
5	Antiques	55	Cooking	105	Jet Skiing
6	Apex Club	56	Counselling	106	Jigsaw Puzzles
7	Aquariums	57	Cricket	107	Kindergarten
8	Archaeology	58	Crochet	108	Kitchen
9	Army Reserve	59	Cross-cultural Mission	109	Knitting
10	Art	60	Crosswords	110	Leather work
11	Astronomy	61	CWA	111	Letter Writing
12	Athletics	62	Dancing	112	Lions Club
13	Australian Rules	63	Disco	113	Macrame
14	Baby Sitting	64	Dog Obedience	114	Maths
15	Ballet Dancing	65	Doll Collecting	115	Meals on Wheels
16	Ballroom Dancing	66	Doll Making	116	Mechanics
17	Baseball	67	Drama	117	Model Railways
18	Basketball	68	Dressmaking	118	Motor Cycles
19	Bee Keeping	69	Driving	119	Motor Racing
20	Bible Study	70	Drumming	120	Netball
21	Bicycling	71	Early Childhood Activity	121	Nutrition
22	Billiards	72	Education	122	Old Time Dancing
23	Bird Ornithology	73	Electronics	123	Opera
24	Bonsai	74	Embroidery	124	Orchid Growing
25	Book Collecting	75	Fancywork	125	Organ Music
26	Book reading	76	Farming	126	Painting
27	Bowls	77	Fine China	127	Paper Serviettes
28	Boxing	78	Fishing	128	Patchwork
29	Boys Brigade	79	Flower Arranging	129	Pen Friendships
30	Bridge	80	Flying	130	Pets
31	Brownies	81	French Polishing	131	Photography
32	Building/Carpentry	82	Fund Raising	132	Physical Culture
33	Bushwalking	83	Gardening	133	Physiology
34	Cake Icing	84	Gem Hunting	134	Picture Framing
35	Calligraphy	85	Girl Guides	135	Playdough
36	Canoeing	86	Girls Brigade	136	Playgroup
37	Camping	87	Gliding	137	Poetry
38	Caravaning	88	Golf	138	Politics
39	Car Care	89	Grass Skiing	139	Pot Plants
40	Card Games	90	Guitar	140	Pottery
41	C B Radio	91	Guns	141	Prayer Groups
42	Cell Groups	92	Gymnastics	142	Prayer Counselling
43	Charity/Voluntary Work	93	Handyman	143	Problem Solving
44	Chess	94	Hang Gliding	144	Public Speaking
45	Children	95	Highland Dancing	145	Radio
46	China Painting	96	History	146	Rap Dancing
47	Chocolate Making	97	Hockey	147	Records
48	Christian Education	98	Horse Riding	148	Rodeos
49	Church Activities	99	Hydroponic Gardening	149	Rotary Club
50	Cinema	100	Indoor Bowls	150	Rowing

151	Running	169	Spinning	187	Travel
152	Rugby League	170	Spoon Collecting	188	Trumpet
153	Sailing	171	Square Dancing	189	Upholstery
154	School P & C	172	Squash	190	Vintage Cars
155	Scouts	173	Stamps	191	Visiting Family
156	Screen Printing	174	Study Groups	192	Volleyball
157	Scuba Diving	175	Surfing	193	Walking
158	Sewing	176	Swimming	194	Water Skiing
159	Shooting	177	Table Tennis	195	Wood Carving
160	Shortwave Radio	178	Tap Dancing	196	Woodwork
161	Singing	179	Tapestry	197	Wrestling
162	Skateboarding	180	Tatting	198	Writing
163	Skating	181	Television	199	Yachting
164	Skiing	182	Tennis	200	Youth Activities
165	Sky Diving	183	Ten Pin Bowling		
166	Soccer	184	Theatre		
167	Softball	185	Theology		
168	Souvenir Collecting	186	Time & Motion Study		

The Leader's Goldmine by Geoff Waugh, © The Joint Board of Christian Education, 1990. Used with permission.

Gifts check list

This list gives you a simple way of checking to see what God is already doing in your life. You can identify some of the gifts you see in yourself.

It's a simple self-assessment guide adapted from similar questionnaires. Give yourself a score on each statement from 5 (strong) to 1 or 0 (weak). Avoid too many scores of 3! Then add your scores in the table to get totals for each line.

Your highest scores will indicate some areas of strength or gifting, as you see it. You could also get a friend to score you as they see you and you could do that for them. Remember this provides a very general guide. You are growing, and other gifts or strengths will emerge as you grow.

This list is also printed in the Serendipity Resources study book *Gifts of the Spirit* by Geoff Waugh.

Gifts check list

Scoring: 5 = strong, to 1 or 0 = weak

1 I like to affirm people.

2 I am good at listening.

3 I love to explain things clearly.

4 I like talking to a group about Jesus.

5 I sense what God is saying to a group.

6 I enjoy witnessing.

7 I give generously to God's work.

8 I choose to live simply for the Kingdom.

9 I am good at organising.

10 I have compassion for people in need.

11 I often pray with sick and hurting people.

12 I am helpful and adaptable.

13 I like doing things for others.

14 I enjoy having visitors or guests.

15 I relate well to other cultures.

16 I often give a lead in discussions.

17 I usually feel courageous in serving God.

18 I sense spiritual oppression quickly.

19 I have strong faith in God's promises.

20 I enjoy praying with people.

21 I find ways to encourage others.

22 I relate to others easily.

23 I love teaching Bible truths.

24 I like preparing messages from the Bible.

25 I get insights or impressions from God.

26 I love helping people to become Christians.

27 I use my resources freely for Christian work.

28 I give away my goods to help the needy.

29 I plan things well.

30 I feel deeply for lonely people.

31 I bring peace to troubled people.

32 I like being helpful.

33 I am active in serving others.

34 I have an open home.

35 I enjoy mixing across cultural groups.

36 I am often chosen leader in a group.

37 I like taking risks for God.

38 I detect spiritual opposition readily.

39 I act in faith on the Spirit's leading.

40 I see my prayers answered regularly.

41 I love building others up, not knocking them.

42 I care about people and like to help them.

43 I like mastering and explaining truth.

44 I find my messages bless others.

45 I get impressions or pictures from the Lord.

46 I have led people to faith in Christ.

47 I always give more than a tithe.

48 I gladly do without many material goods.

49 I easily set goals and work for them.

50 I relate closely with hurting people.

51 I pray for the sick and see them helped.

52 I am happy doing practical work.

53 I see needs and do something to help.

54 I like having people drop in on me.

55 I adapt well to different lifestyles.

56 I put plenty of thought into things I lead.

57 I often speak boldly in Jesus' name.

58 I have taken authority over evil spirits.

59 I believe in God's word very strongly.

60 I often tune into God through the day.

61 I work at encouraging people.

62 I really care about people.

63 I am patient in helping others understand.

64 I have a strong call to preach in some way.

65 I often get a word or leading from the Lord.

66 I love talking to non-Christians about Jesus.

67 I give gladly to many Christian ministries.

68 I am happy on a small income.

69 I pay attention to details in organisation.

70 I like to get alongside people in need.

71 I take time to comfort and pray for the sick.

72 I help people in practical ways.

73 I am fulfilled when I serve others.

74 I love having people at my place.

75 I enjoy making friends with foreigners.

76 I often delegate work to others in teams.

77 I am willing to stand up for Jesus anytime.

78 I have commanded evil powers to leave.

79 I step out in faith and see things happen.

80 I pray for others regularly.

SCORING TABLE

Write your scores for each sentence then total them horizontally in the last column.

1	____	21	____	41	____	61	____	____	A
2	____	22	____	42	____	62	____	____	B
3	____	23	____	43	____	63	____	____	C
4	____	24	____	44	____	64	____	____	D
5	____	25	____	45	____	65	____	____	E
6	____	26	____	46	____	66	____	____	F
7	____	27	____	47	____	67	____	____	G
8	____	28	____	48	____	68	____	____	H
9	____	29	____	49	____	69	____	____	I
10	____	30	____	50	____	70	____	____	J
11	____	31	____	51	____	71	____	____	K
12	____	32	____	52	____	72	____	____	L
13	____	33	____	53	____	73	____	____	M
14	____	34	____	54	____	74	____	____	N
15	____	35	____	55	____	75	____	____	O
16	____	36	____	56	____	76	____	____	P
17	____	37	____	57	____	77	____	____	Q
18	____	38	____	58	____	78	____	____	R
19	____	39	____	59	____	79	____	____	S
20	____	40	____	60	____	80	____	____	T

AREAS OF GIFTS

A ENCOURAGEMENT — supporting and affirming others

B PASTORAL — caring for people and helping them

C TEACHING — imparting truth to help people grow

D PREACHING — proclaiming God's word

E PROPHETIC — revealing insights received from God

F EVANGELISM — introducing people to Jesus

G GIVING — spirit of liberality and generosity

H VOLUNTARY POVERTY — going without for the sake of others

I ADMINISTRATION — helping plans to fulfilment

J MERCY — compassion and care for others

K HEALING — bringing wholeness to hurting people

L HELPING — assisting others in their work

M SERVICE — finding ways to serve other people

N HOSPITALITY — open heart and home for people

O MISSIONARY — cross-cultural ministry

P LEADERSHIP — involving others in ministry

Q COURAGE — gifted with boldness or authority

R DISCERNMENT — awareness of spiritual forces

S FAITH — firm belief leading to action

T INTERCESSION — commitment in prayer for others

Bible passages on these gifts are given in the group study book *Living in the Spirit* by Geoff Waugh (JBCE) and fuller studies on each one, plus other gifts, in *27 Spiritual Gifts* by Robert Hillman (JBCE).

The Leader's Goldmine by Geoff Waugh, © The Joint Board of Christian Education, 1990. Used with permission.

Ideas for all ages together

**Activities involving young children
and others
Activities involving older children and
others
Family and church family
questionnaires
Useful teaching activities
ABC of resource ideas
Simulation activities and games
Simulation game: Build my church**

Family Worship (at church and in the home) and learning activities which involve all ages can help people relate together across generations. These ideas can be integrated into church and home life, such as in:

Family Worship — home devotions, church family services, worship in the round;
Learning Activities — at home, in church school, and family camps.

Activities involving young children and others

Audio-visuals: watching, listening, commenting, participating, making

Banners: planning, making, using; sheets, hessian, calico, felt, old curtains

Bible stories: listening, telling, discussing, acting, illustrating

Bible study: adapting questions and activities to mixed ages

Books: looking, reading, finding pictures, discussing, exploring

Brainstorm: sharing ideas, record these on cassettes, paper, chalkboard

Charades: drama and mime, spoken or silent, mixed or same age

Charts and flip charts: watching, discussing, making, illustrating

Choral speaking and singing: small or large groups, whole congregation

Clay modelling: scenes, shapes, people, objects, stories

Collage: making individual or group sheet using pictures, headlines, cut-outs

Collecting and sorting objects: individual and group sharing

Colouring: pictures, printing, signs, designs

Contests: spoken, drawn, action; individually, in teams and groups

Conversation: sharing ideas, interests, discussion, planning

Cooking and cleaning: participation in the process and results

Craft: demonstrations and practice, e.g. candles, kites, models

Creative activities: spontaneous or prepared; note ideas for *Program Emphases*

Crests: designing and making personal or family crests

Drama: spontaneous or prepared; participating and watching

Drawing: individual and group; small and large sheets, chalkboards

Dancing and movement: indoors and outdoors; spontaneous and prepared

Eating: breaking bread together; sharing fruit, drinks, food

Evaluating: noting likes and dislikes, successful activities

Excursions: on foot, by car, bus or train; brief walk or longer outing

Films and slides: watching, making, discussing, reproducing

Games: indoors and outdoors; note ideas for *Sporting Program emphases*

Groups: working in families, ages, mixed and extended family clusters

Imagining and pretending: thinking, day dreaming, meditating, talking, action

Jokes and yarns: swapping, sharing, guessing, laughing together

Listening: music recordings, singing, stories, sounds

Magazines: looking, reading, tearing, cutting, arranging

Maps: drawing, making and using; paper, cardboard, papier mache, relief maps

Masks: making and wearing; using in drama, speaking, story telling

Meals: buffet, sandwich, basket lunch/tea, hotpot, barbecue, breakfast

Memorising: texts, mottos, proverbs, verses, songs, rhymes

Mime: spontaneous and prepared; individual and groups, mixed or same ages

Mobile making: family, groups, individuals; pictures, designs, words

Model making: paper, cardboard, papier mache, wire, Lego

Modelling: Plasticine, clay, play dough, dough

Montage: 3D creations, recycling waste materials, personal and group

Music: listening and making; percussion band, instruments, records

Open-ended stories and plays: individuals, groups, families complete

Over-head projector: designing and making slides, rolls; words, pictures

Painting: small and large sheets; individual and group work

Picnics: outings, barbecues, sandwiches; parks, playgrounds, homes

Planning: sharing ideas and interests; families working together

Plasticine: scenes, shapes, people, objects, stories

Posters: for books, walls, flip charts, banners, sandwich boards

Prayer: note ideas on prayers; individual, family, group

Projects: individual, family and group; books, sheets, tasks, presentations

Puppets: hand, finger, paper bag, socks, papier mache, string

Puzzles: spoken and written; flip charts, books, boards, action

Quizzes: spoken and written; individual and group or family

Reading: illustrated, acted, individual and groups

Reciting: individual and choral

Recording: ideas, comments, interviews, songs, sound effects

Riddles: spoken and written; competitions, collections, composing

Role play: past, present and future situations; role reversals

Sharing experiences: discoveries, family activities, ideas, hopes

Show and tell: object talks, interest centres, swap shop

Simulation games and activities: roles and personal responses or involvement; note ideas on *Simulation activities and games.*

Singing: together, in families, groups, choirs; planned and free choice

Values clarification: individual and group tasks, family planning

Walking: indoors and outdoors, exploring, exercises, clusters

Watching TV.: informally or as part of a structured learning experience

Worship: formal and informal; planned by individuals, families or groups

Worship centres: displays, arrangements, themes, objects, expression work

Writing: tracing shapes, copying, helping each other, project work

Activities involving older children and others

These learning activities may be used with older children and adults. They may also be part of family worship, camps and teaching sessions. Note *Ideas for Building Relationships*, and many activities involving young children which can also be used with any age group.

Audio-tapes: played to whole group, or by individuals; guidance for study, group discussion, practical work; resource for open education

Bible study: individual and groups; spoken and written; shared ideas; note *Bible study methods*

Books: study, reviews, summaries, quizzes, tests, skim reading, illustrating, comparing, annotating

Brainstorm: spontaneous suggestions are received uncritically to generate new ideas, problem solving and decision making

Buzz groups: small clusters of people to discuss a topic or question or complete a task and report to the whole group

Case discussion: real or simulated problems are analysed to suggest or discover alternative solutions and decisions

Controlled discussion: students raise questions or comment but the discussion is controlled by the teacher(s)

Counselling: real or simulated consultation with a counsellor about personal problems and concerns

Circular response: everyone in the group responds to a question or task briefly in turn

Demonstrations: a task or skill is performed while others watch in order to learn the process

Drama: various forms of acting, prepared or

spontaneous, which involve people in representing situations in dramatic ways

Encounter group: group members discuss their relationships with each other to increase sensitivity, awareness and ability

Evaluation: any assessment process by individuals or the group which attempts to determine the effectiveness of what has been done

Extension education: a form of external study or home study which involves group work as part of the learning process and includes assignments

Films and filmstrips: 16mm and 8mm films and filmstrips used (sometimes made by the group) to focus learning and illustrate topics

Free-group discussion: the topic and direction of discussion is determined by the group while teachers or leaders observe

Group tutorial: the topic and direction are given but the group work, content and discussion depend on the group

Individual tutorial: teaching devoted to one person with interaction between the participants in the process

Individual task: a problem or activity is given to the whole group to be performed by each individual (e.g. writing an assignment)

Lecture: An uninterrupted talk on a topic which may or may not involve the whole learning period

Lecturette: a brief form of a lecture, often given by students, usually followed by questions and discussion

Micro-teaching: the demonstration of a skill or process (often video taped) by a student or students, which is observed and discussed

Practicals: laboratory type experiences in which the group participates in the learning process or task by attempting it

Preaching: inspirational lecturing to impart knowledge and motivate people to grow in relationship with God and others

Problem-centred groups: groups which are each given a specific task to discuss and report on or complete

Programmed Learning: a series of tasks (usually questions in a book or on cards) each of which must be answered and checked before proceeding

Projects: individual or group tasks involving practical skills which are usually submitted on paper when completed

Radio lessons: broadcasted lessons (sometimes involving response on two-way transceivers) usually requiring listening and writing skills

Reading: individual or group task often involving the use of library or text books, including skim or speed reading

Recording: use of tape recording, especially cassettes, for individual or group use, as for revision, interviews, and comments

Role Play: including sociodrama, where people act social roles and freely dramatise them in the group

Role reversal: a form of role play in which people act out opposite roles from their usual ones, eg. young/old, husband/wife, parent/child

Seminar: group discussion introduced by the presentation of the topic in a lecturette, essay or other introductory activity

Simulation games: a real situation is duplicated in its essential elements in the form of a game or problem. Note *Simulation games and activities.*

Step-by-step discussion: a carefully prepared sequence of issues and questions to guide the discussion through required information

Step-by-step lecture: a lecture or series of lecturettes organised around topics which are talked about and followed by brief discussion or activity

Syndicate method: syndicate groups of about six people work on the same or related problems with some teacher contact, and write a joint report

Symposium: People represent different points of view on a topic followed by group discussion and interaction

Synetics: a form of brainstorm in which people from diverse backgrounds contribute ideas to produce a creative solution to the issue

Task group: each small group is given a particular task to consider and fulfil, usually reporting results to the whole group when completed

Team teaching: two or more people co-operate in the planning and leading of sessions combining their skills in team work

Television (including video-tapes and closed circuit T.V.) these offer a wide range of teaching opportunities including micro-teaching

Values clarification: questions and exercises, often in brief activities, to help individuals and groups determine priorities and values

Workshop: a development of the seminar in which participants work together on the topic or issue to produce relevant ideas, information or materials

Writing: individual or group activities in a wide range of tasks including creative writing to compose verse, songs, prose or notes

Family and church family questionnaires

Select from these questions the ones most helpful to your group, such as for group sharing, family activities, or church planning. Work in family groups or small clusters of 4 to 5 people. Allow about 10 minutes for each question you use.

Family life

1. What do you like most about your family life?

2. What hobby do you enjoy most in your family?

3. What do you like to do with your family?

4. What is a Saturday family activity you would like?

5. What is a motto you would like for your family?

6. What would you like to be doing at 40 or 80?

7. What was one of your happiest family times?

8. Where would you really like to live for the next five years?

9. If you received $10,000 as a family gift, how would you like to spend it?

10. How do you feel right now about your family?

11. How does your family life fit in with school or work?

12. What is one talent God has given you which you can use in family life?

13. What is one thing you like in each person in your home?

14. What do you like most about your involvement in your family?

15. If you had one month to do anything, what would you like to do as a family?

16. What family recreation do you like?

17. What embarrasses you in your family?

18. What is a quality you like most in your family life?

19. Describe happy family life?

20. What do you do that involves full concentration in family activity?

21. What feelings do you have most trouble expressing in your family?

22. What is a favourite song in your home?

23. What music do you like being played at home?

24. What makes a happy home?

25. What material possession do you value most?

26. If your house was on fire what would you grab as you left?

27. What do you do at home when you feel lonely?

28. What is family life all about for you?

29. What does it mean for Jesus to be Lord in your home?

30. How can you serve God best at home?

Church family

1. What do you like most about church life?

2. What do you like least about church life?

3. What is most important to you about the church?

4. If you could change something at church, what would you do?

5. What would you like to see happen more in church life?

6. What gives you most enjoyment as a family at church?

7. What is one dream you have for your church?

8. What was one of the happiest times at church?

9. What is the best advice you remember receiving at church?

10. How does church life help your family life?

11. Who at church has been especially helpful to you?

12. What would you like to happen in a church home group?

13. What is a vision or dream you have for your church?

14. How can you enjoy church family life more?

15. What hymn or chorus do you especially like, and why?

16. What does serving God mean for you?

17. How did you become a Christian?

18. What does "life abundant" (John 10:10) mean for you?

19. How would you like to serve God in the church?

20. What challenges you most about Jesus?

21. What does peace mean for you?

22. What makes you feel close to God?

23. What does "grow in grace" (2 Peter 3:18) mean for you?

24. How can others help you grow as a Christian?

25. What is a favourite verse or Bible passage for you?

26. What do you want God to do for you?

27. What would you like people to pray about for you?

28. What do you want to do for God?

29. What would you like to pray for now?

30. How can people in your group help you now?

Useful teaching activities

Adapt and expand these ideas to suit your group.

Read — modern versions of the Bible
— resource books and magazines (Bible Dictionary, Bible Atlas)
— students' books, assignment sheets, notes
— creative work done by other students

Write — answers to set questions, incomplete sentences, puzzles
— the story or study from a participant's point of view
— a paraphrase in your own words
— a parable or similar situation today
— a play or dramatic version of the study or modern parallel
— a diary of the main events, or a personal diary
— a journal of ideas, opinions, reactions, feelings
— a poem, verse, or jingle; free form verse
— a cinquain poem:

Title:	_____	one word
Words to describe:	___ ___	two words
Words of action:	___ ___ ___	three words
Words of feeling:	___ ___ ___ ___	four words
Conclusion:	_____	one word

— a Haiku Poem
3 lines with a total of 17 syllables: 5, 7, 5
e.g. Jesus is our Lord (5)
His message is eternal (7)
Heaven is his love (5)
— a song, e.g. using a well known tune e.g.
There were twelve disciples Jesus called to help him,
Simon, Peter, Andrew, James, his brother John,
Philip, Thomas, Matthew, James the son of Alphaeus,
Thaddaeus, Simon, Judas, and Bartholomew.
He has called us too; he has called us too;
We are his disciples, I am one, are you?
He has called us too; he has called us too;
We are his disciples, we his work must do.
(From Matthew 10:1-4 to tune 'Bringing in the Sheaves')
— summaries, notes, illustrations on slides, OHP (overhead projector), flip charts, posters, chalkboard, banners
— time charts and diagrams, eg. this time line:

— mnemonics, e.g. *pictures* for numbers 1-10

1 is bun	NO OTHER GODS — a bun shaped like a god.
2 is shoe	NO IDOLS — shoes hanging on Hindu idol's feet.
3 is tree	NO SWEARING — tree falls on lumberjack's foot and !!!
4 is door	REMEMBER SABBATH — a church doorway
5 is hive	HONOUR PARENTS — bees at home in hive
6 is sticks	NO MURDER — murderer clubs victim with sticks
7 is heaven	NO ADULTERY — sultan gets wives on magic carpet in sky
8 is gate	NO STEALING — horse thief opens paddock gate
9 is vine	NO LIES — vineyard owner lies about size of harvest
10 is hen	NO COVETING — glutton covets neighbour's hen for dinner

See — slides, film strip, film (Super 8, 16mm), T.V., video, and compare with Bible; tell the story; write a script; discuss; use as motivation for creative work
— pictures, words, from magazine to illustrate topic, interests, values
— OHP (overhead projector), chalkboard, flip chart used by teacher to present information and summaries, to record student responses, reports, used by student to present small group work, to create visual work
— life in action, by excursions, visiting relevant places

Do — draw, illustrate
— make models (paper, cardboard, papier mache, mixed media)
— make and use puppets (finger, hand, glove, papier mache, string)
— dramatise, role play
— creative movement, dance, mime
— make a project (collage, montage, mural, freize, posters, banners)
— plan and complete a group task (help aged, sick, visit homes)
— walk and explore
— show and tell

2000	1000	+	1000	2000

Gen. 1-11 ├──┼──┼──┼──┼──┼──┼──┼──┤ Rev. 20-21

Abraham   David   Jesus   East/West   Present
                                     Churches
    Moses   Daniel   Bible   Ref.

- play games, simulations
- sing (without or with words in books, on sheets, OHP, charts)
- listen to recordings (singing, music, words, sounds)

Speak
- tell story
- lecturette
- read aloud
- record on tape (reading, plays, stories, interviews)
- interview people
- discuss

Continue to add your own ideas.

Some useful resources

Equipment:

Video camera and recorder, TV, video tapes — home made or rented

Movie projector and screen, 16mm or Super 8 films — home made or rented

Slide and film strip projector, slides and filmstrips

OHP (overhead projector) and transparencies — bought or blank

Record player and records, compact disks

Cassette recorder and audio tapes

Musical instruments

Chalkboard, whiteboard

Flannelgraph board and materials

Supplies

Bibles — different translations

Resource books — Bible dictionary, Bible commentaries, Bible atlas, Bible story books, story books, biographies

Hymns and songs — books, sheets, OHP transparencies

Paper, cardboard, newsprint, note books, loose leaf books

Pencils, biros, felt pens, OHP pens, crayons, coloured chalk

Scissors, paste, starch, papers and magazines

Dress-up materials — old hats and clothes

Flip chart, chart, posters

Scrap paper

A B C of resource ideas

This list can be used for a handy alphabetical file as well as for an index list or contents of your loose leaf resource book.

Activities — group work
Bible studies and stories
Camping
Devotions
Essays — assignments
Folk arts — songs — music
Games
Handcraft
Illustrations — stories

Jokes — humour
Kids — children
Liturgies
Media
Note
Outlines
Program ideas
Quotations
Relational ideas

Simulations — values clarification
Teaching materials
Unfinished tasks — dreams and visions
Verse — poetry
Worship
X-rays — photography
Youth
Zion file — historical data

Simulation activities and games

Simulation activities and games provide a powerful means of teaching if used well. They involve people at a feeling level, sometimes deeply. Often they are very creative.

You need to explain the basic rules or guidelines carefully before beginning. Then at the end you need to de-role. That involves stepping out of the activity or game, and usually needs a time to reflect on it together. Use the third person when you de-role (e.g. 'The minister was . . .' or 'How did the minister feel when . . .' etc.). Try to avoid carrying on the roles in the second person (e.g. avoid 'You were . . .' or 'How did you feel when . . .').

Many useful books describe various simulation activities or games. Some are simple; some very complex. The ideas here are basic ones to help get you going. With a little practice you will soon create your own.

These activities are divided for convenience into ones in which you play a role or represent someone else and ones in which you are yourself.

Play a role

1. Role Play

A small play or sketch in which you spontaneously act your role. Sometimes it helps to pin labels on people in the role play so that others know who they are immediately.

Some examples: a church meeting, Bible stories, common events (e.g. showing kindness), a community group, an event in history or in the future.

Try these approaches:

a. Choose a theme. Get your group to prepare a role play on the theme (e.g. forgiveness). Divide a large group into smaller sub-groups and note the variety as each sub-group prepares something on the theme.

b. Bible Story. Get the group or sub-groups to prepare and present small plays on the Bible story or scene.

c. Bible scene. Imagine a scene which may (or may not) have happened. Depict it in a play, e.g. observers at an event (like the cross, Jesus' miracles, spectators in Jerusalem, Abraham's servants, David's followers, etc.).

d. History scene. Depict some event in history, or how people may have reacted then, e.g. St. Francis, Wilberforce.

e. Current events. Take a topical issue and depict it in play form.

f. Church group. Select appropriate roles like the minister, elders, youth, ladies, etc. to present an issue.

2. Interviews

The group could interview a person or panel, or the interview can be conducted by one person (e.g. a reporter or a church representative).

Some suggestions:

a. Bible character. Interview Abraham, David, Peter, Paul, or anyone the person chooses to be.

b. Historical character. People could choose someone they admire or know a lot about.

c. Current personality. Focus on the news or world events.

d. Church personality. Question someone whose role is the minister, youth leader, visitor, etc.

3. Role reversal

Swap roles and act how you see it, e.g. parent/child, husband/wife, leader/follower, adult/youth, over 30/under 30, clergy/laity, Christian/agnostic, etc. This can be done in pairs or in groups. It often touches some deep feelings and needs careful de-roling, like 'How did the parent feel . . .?'/'How did the child feel . . .?'

4. Counselling or Helping

Act the counsellor or helper. The client's problem or concern can be imagined or real but should involve real issues. This can be very powerful in teaching counselling or helping skills.

5. Presentation

A person or group could present information or a message, prepared or spontaneous. A person or group from the Bible, history, current events, or the Church could bring their message or tell of events affecting them. A large group could be divided into small sub-groups for various presentations.

6. Crisis

A small group, or sub-groups of a large one, must solve a crisis with each person acting out a particular role. Some examples: a Biblical crisis like the disciples after the crucifixion or Paul's missionary band facing persecution; a crisis in history like Christians being imprisoned or breaking away from traditional values; a current crisis like how to handle an aggressive and oppressive military dictatorship; your group faces possible death (e.g. nuclear bomb, plane crash, lost in desert safari, etc.) and must decide what to do.

Some roles could be adults, youth, children, clergy, rich, poor, student, engaged, married, parents, handyman, business executive, soldier, doctor, nurse, Christian, atheist, handicapped person, and so on.

7. Allocation

Everyone in the group is allocated a lot in life or set situation, and must do the best they can in that circumstance.

Some situations: rich and poor eat at separate tables; servants and masters in a room together; Christians try to witness in various ways to different kinds of unbelievers; dogmatic people discuss the Bible with open-minded people; church business meeting where some are allocated traditionalists, some radicals, some peace keepers, some who just want to pray about it.

8. Case studies

Real or simulated situations or problems are presented to the group for them to solve. Each person in the group must respond according to their given role, e.g. clergy, doctor, youth, millionaire, social worker, and so on.

9. Action

You can simulate many situations involving action or acting, e.g. plays, drama, musicals, operetta, singing.

10. Try your own

Adapt these ideas to suit your own situation or needs.

Be yourself

1. Adapt roles

Many of the above suggestions can also be adapted without roles, so that you are yourself in that situation.

Some examples:

a. Prepare a simulation on a theme in which you are yourself, e.g. showing forgiveness, planning ahead.

b. Work through a current event or church issue in a meeting or task group in which you participate as yourself.

c. Interview a person or people, for real.

d. Counselling or helping with a real situation as a demonstration or learning practice.

e. Micro-teaching in a real situation in your group, e.g. practise or demonstrate leading your group or teaching in it.

f. Present a theme or message in simulation form in which you act yourself, e.g. youth group in action.

g. Participate in a crisis situation where each person in the group is responding as they would, or think they would, in that situation.

h. Allocate a lot in life or set situation to the group, but everyone acts as themselves in that particular circumstance.

i. Be yourself in a case study looking at your life or present situation.

j. Participate in a group which examines a real or imagined case study, but don't act a role; be yourself.

2. Relate
Use the *Ideas for building relationships* in this book as a game or activity to help you relate together. There are many ways to do this outlined at the beginning of that section.

3. Hot seat
The group interviews a person. Only ask questions; no discussion during the simulation. The person being interviewed always has the right to pass, i.e. not answer a question.

4. Core group
You are a core group in your church and must decide how each person in the group can best serve God in the church. This can be very powerful, and needs to be affirming.

5. Caring group
You are a group set up by your church to look at ways to care for others. Plan together.

6. Task group
Your group has been given, or chooses, a particular task to plan and organise. Work on that together.

7. Micro-teaching
Practise a segment of an activity and then discuss it. Keep it brief. This is useful for practice sessions (e.g. teaching, counselling, church groups, personal skills like speaking or leading and so on). After the play use evaluation questions like 'What was most effective?' and 'What could be improved?'

8. Action games
You can simulate many situations by involving people in appropriate actions or activities.

Some examples: various eating experiences (poor, rich, international foods, Passover, love feast); trust walk (blindfolded and led by the hand or by spoken directions); trust fall (you stand rigid with your eyes closed in a small circle and fall, trusting one or two to catch you); group support (lay back and be lifted on the hands of the group up above their heads); cradled (3 to 5 pairs hold hands facing each other in two lines and you lie on their arms while they rock you gently); singing, dramas and operettas depicting life as you see it.

9. Table games
Many table games simulate real life (e.g. 'Monopoly' and trading; 'Snakes and Ladders' and morality — snakes for bad qualities, and ladders for good). Some recent games give even more complex simulations, including video games. Many board games depict a journey to a particular destination.

Have you tried to play Monopoly with Christian values like co-operation and helping others? What happens to games played with Christian values as the guiding rules?

10. Quizzes
A quiz or puzzle can be turned into a simulation also. Individual or teams can compete, or co-operate. One example is Bible Cricket where one team asks questions of the other team till they get them all out. A correct answer scores a run; an incorrect answer or none bowls that person out.

11. Paper games
A huge range of games involve pencil/pen/biro and paper, including games in which you score.

You could rate people according to selected values, e.g. Joseph's brothers or Jesus' disciples or Paul's team rated from 1-5 on qualities like courage, faithfulness, humility or leadership.

Some of the Relationship activities in this book also make interesting values clarifications or simulation exercises.

The following simulation game 'Build My Church' involves scoring in various ways, and this type of scoring can be used for many statements like the ones in this game.

12. Variety
You can adapt many simulation activities or games in many ways. The following example 'Build My Church' suggests some ways using scoring, a continuum, and values voting.

Simulation game: 'Build my Church' Matthew 16:18

Rules

This game simulates a church council or planning meeting. It has educational value.

The aim of the game is to discover what others think about the church, and how well you can estimate their ideas.

Procedure: Play in groups of 2-5. A copy of the statements will be needed in each group. Each person in turn selects *one statement* from each category and ranks their level of agreement with it by writing any number from 5 to 1:

    5 — strongly agree
    4 — agree
    3 — no opinion, neutral
    2 — disagree
    1 — strongly disagree

All the others in the group estimate what that person's number will be, and write that down. Then results are compared. Your score is the difference between your guess, and the person's number. If you guessed correctly, you score 0. *Complete the round of one category* in your group before moving on to another.

Scoring: Write the names of the others in your group along a line leaving space for a column of ten scores beneath each name. Enter your scores after each turn, *completing all scores for Category 1 first*. After completing all categories, total your scores under each person's name, then add these totals. The winner has the smallest total score.

More important than the scores will be what you learn about each other, and about the church. After each turn, you may benefit from discussing your *interpretations* of the statements.

Additional scoring: If you wish, you can then note the sum of the group's personal totals for each person, and for each category. Concerning persons, you can discover whose ideas are best known — or most predictable! Concerning categories, you can discover the areas of most and least understanding by your group of the attitudes you have in these categories.

Alternative games

1. 'Build My Church' statements may be used with a large group by indicating personal positions on a *continuum*.

Select appropriate statements, then get everyone in the group to stand in the position representing their personal opinion, e.g. along a wall, from strongly agree (left) to strongly disagree (right). Individuals could then give reasons for their position by:

    (a) talking in pairs with someone near you;
    (b) talking with a few near you in groups;
    (c) talking in pairs with someone differing from you;
    (d) talking with a few differing from you in groups;
    (e) give personal reasons to the whole group.

Be sensitive to personal feelings and opinions.

2. Similar to Alternative (1), but using *Values Voting*: people remain seated and vote on each statement used:

    (a) strongly agree — wave hand
    (b) agree — hand up
    (c) no opinion, neutral — fold arms
    (d) disagree — thumbs down
    (e) strongly disagree — thumbs down stirring

This is useful for quick responses from any group, and immediately shows the diversity in any group. Some people could be asked to give reasons for their personal vote.

Statements

A. INSTITUTIONAL

1. Western Christianity is heretical.

2. Our traditions nullify God's Word.

3. Denominations are the best way to organise the church.

4. The Charismatic Movement is dangerous.

5. Home cells are vital for renewal.

6. Middle-class Christianity makes the church ineffective.

7. The Ecumenical Movement is pointless.

8. Institutional Christianity exists mainly to keep existing.

9. Most denominations will phase out next century.

10. Denominational departments are mainly a waste of money.

B. MINISTRY

1. One minister per church is preferable.

2. Elders should determine policy in a church.

3. Every church service should have a sermon.

4. Ordination should be for pastoral ministry.

5. Ordination is becoming meaningless.

6. Women should have access to all church positions.

7. Team ministries are essential.

8. Early church miracles are possible in your church.

9. First Century church power is equally available today.

10. Specialists are preferably in ministry.

C. WORSHIP

1. Everyone should participate in worship as they feel led.

2. Organs are preferable in worship.

3. Instruments are preferable in church services.

4. Hymn books are too restrictive.

5. Spontaneous worship is preferable.

6. Read liturgies are necessary.

7. Ancient English often makes worship artificial.

8. Worship services should usually be about one hour.

9. Religion is the opiate of the people.

10. Traditional services inoculate people against worship.

D. FELLOWSHIP
1. Homes should be used more than church buildings in church life.

2. Fellowship teas are usually superficial.

3. Cell groups are vital for growth.

4. It is best to mix age groups in the church.

5. Men's groups are essential for outreach.

6. Women's groups are vital for fellowship.

7. Families should organise some church services.

8. Families should be able to participate in church services.

9. Homes limited to nuclear families are sub-Christian.

10. Regular family devotions usually enrich family life.

E. EDUCATION
1. Sunday School is usually ineffective.

2. Christian Education is the responsibility of the home.

3. Religious Education in schools is best taught by school staff.

4. Church procedures severely limit educational growth.

5. The Authorised Version hinders knowledge of God's Word.

6. Cassettes and paperbacks are basic tools for Christian Education.

7. Most Christians are stunted spiritually.

8. Religious Education in schools should be mainly Comparative Religions.

9. Bible exams are advisable for children.

10. All Christians should seriously study other religions.

F. MISSION
1. Mission is best left to the professionals.

2. Home visits are most effective for evangelism.

3. Face to face friendship evangelism is best.

4. Mass evangelism is the most successful outreach.

5. Church growth is mainly a sociological phenomenon.

6. Mass media should get most of our money for envangelism.

7. Cassettes provide powerful outreach today.

8. The local parish is the best base for mission.

9. Overseas missions should be abolished.

10. Family life is the most natural means of mission.

G. SERVICE
1. The church should organise social services.

2. Groups of Christians should organise social welfare.

3. All denominations should co-operate in social concerns.

4. Private homes are preferable to social care institutions.

5. Churches should stay out of politics.

6. Christians usually over-simplify social evils.

7. Only specialists should plan social welfare.

8. Spontaneous caring is the best answer to social needs.

9. Life Line should include non-Christian telephone counsellors.

10. Christians should demand social action through governments.

H. PLANT
1. Pews are ineffective.

2. Church buildings are a waste of money.

3. Money should be spent on decent church buildings.

4. Cathedrals are mainly museums now.

5. The loss of all church property would be beneficial.

6. Community centres are ideal for church life.

7. Church Union is vital to rationalise plant.

8. Far too much time is wasted in maintenance.

9. Church budgets are essential.

10. Denominational leaders need to plan most expenditure.

I. PERSONAL
(Add ten statements of your own, e.g. on local issues)

Ideas for integrated studies on themes

The Great Experiment
Prayer
Relationship
Good news
The church
Mission
Finding new life
Living new life
Faith alive
Great chapters — Old Testament
Great chapters — New Testament
Jesus

Each integrated study follows a theme for a month, covering these topics:
These topics can be used in any order, or you can select only one for a month's study. They provide you with 11 months of group studies.
Some themes fit naturally together, especially **Finding new life** and **Living new life** which are adapted from readings in the Life in the Spirit seminars.
Each topic enables you to integrate the group studies with personal, family and church studies. You could begin with **The great experiment** as an optional part of the study on Prayer and then work through each theme. If, for example, you began in February (after the summer vacation in Australia) then you could study Relationship in March, Good News in April (around Easter), The Church in May (around Pentecost), and so on, concluding with the study of Jesus (at Christmas). Most detail is given in the earlier studies. By the time your group has worked through them you do not need the same detail repeated continually in later studies. You can, of course, use any study at any time, and select the sections which fit your situation. Many groups use only the personal and group sections. The family sections can be adapted for use in Sunday School or for children's activities following the same themes as the adult studies.
Each topic includes four studies: personal, group, family and church.

Personal study offers suggestions for daily study of the seven readings each week. Readings are brief. Anyone can add them to their usual routine easily. You gain most from these studies by using a note book or diary for brief journal entries.

Group study outlines suggestions for group sharing. You will need one to two hours in your group each week. Homes are ideal. Some groups may meet as adult or youth classes on Sunday. Large groups should work in sub-groups or small groups of no more than 5 to 10. Adapt the group study to meet your needs. Some groups begin with worship and then move into small groups or cells for sharing and prayer.

Family study provides some suggestions for inter-generational activities involving children. It could take 30 minutes to an hour, depending on the ages of children. Young children need activity in short spans. You could use this to encourage a family devotional time once a week. You may like to try adapting it for Sunday School groups, especially where the theme is used in church services.

Church study gives suggestions for using the theme in informal services or family services. Creative options can be found to adapt these ideas to any church service. The theme can either be introduced on Sunday and followed through during the week, or you can use the church studies to conclude the work done during the week. If you follow lectionary readings you will often find links between some readings and these themes.
Be flexible in using this material. As personal issues are raised they can be considered. If members of a home group, for example, follow the daily readings during the week, you do not need to spend so much time on that but can move quickly into sharing the relevance and meaning of those scriptures for your lives.
A month's theme can also be used for a weekend camp, especially a family camp. Personal study ideas can be used for morning devotions, group study for adults and youth groups, family study for family or children's activities, and church study for worship times. The first of the following integrated studies on themes uses the readings in **The great experiment**. That study can be linked with **The great experiment**, which is how we used it in a lively home group for which these integrated studies were originally written.

The great experiment

In January 1965, Sam Teague, the leader of a young adults group at John Wesley Methodist Church in Florida, asked God to show him how to challenge his group to have a life that matters. The ideas for **The great experiment** came to him as he noted them down for 20 minutes that Sunday morning. Danny Morris, then minister at the church, told the story of how it revolutionised the group and the whole church in his book *A Life that (Really) Matters*. Originally the program was also called 'Wanted: 10 Brave Christians,' and has since spread around the world encouraging Christians to deeper commitment in putting God first in their lives as they follow the program for one month.

The great experiment puts together five spiritual disciplines: prayer, service, tithing, Bible study, and Christian concern for others.

1. Meet once each week to pray together.

This is a time of prayer, sharing and study, each given half an hour. It includes silent as well as voluntary, spoken prayer; sharing of questions and problems as well as discoveries and experiences; and study of helpful books as well as the Bible. Groups are encouraged to keep records of prayer needs and results. The answers from God have been clear and often amazing.

2. Give two hours time each week to God.

Self-surrender is involved in such service. Here is a Beginning List:

1. Visit hospital patients or shut-ins.

2. Visit members of the church to tell them about your experiences.

3. Visit families interested in the church and try to involve them.

4. Be a teacher or helper in a Sunday School class for a month.

5. Join the choir for a month.

6. Visit your neighbourhood for one or two hours to find 'prospects'.

7. Spend an hour visiting two or three church families you do not know.

8. Visit new members of the church to get acquainted.

9. Help provide needed improvements, e.g. furnishings, shelving, curtains.

10. Be a telephone committee of one, contacting people for the church.

11. Promote and maintain a church library during the month.

12. Work in your church office for one or two hours.

13. Work on the grounds of the church property — a continuing need.

14. Visit the homes of visitors to the church.

15. Use your imagination to discover other things the church needs you to do.

3. Give God ¹⁄₁₀ of earnings during this month.

Self-denial is part of tithing. Each person is encouraged to take the tithe out first and pray about how to effectively spend the other ⁹⁄₁₀ of income.

4. Spend from 5.30-6.00 each morning in prayer and the study of Scripture.

The original program required this at 5.30-6.00 each morning, and this is strongly recommended for best results. It affects the whole day.

Self-control is needed for this discipline. Here is the schedule:

10 minutes 5.30-5.40 Read the scripture for the day (see list). Pray and meditate on this scripture. Write out in less than 50 words how this passage applies to your life.

10 minutes 5.40-5.50 Write out one totally unselfish and unexpected act of kindness or generosity that you will do today. Name the person — then act during the day, vigorously and with compassion and love. Keep a written record of (1) the reaction of the person toward whom the kindness is extended, and (2) the effect of this act upon you personally.

10 minutes 5.50-6.00 Write out carefully how you would like to build and develop your life. Go into great detail if you desire. Take your time — be thoughtful and prayerful. One well prayed out and thought out sentence per day would be excellent progress.

Daily scriptures:

(1)	2 Chronicles 7:14	(17)	Isaiah 59:1-3
(2)	James 5:16	(18)	Proverbs 28:9-10
(3)	1 John 3:22	(19)	Matthew 8:23-27
(4)	John 15:6-7	(20)	John 6:47
(5)	Mark 11:24-25	(21)	Ecclesiastes 3:1-8
(6)	Philippians 4:6	(22)	Psalm 55:22
(7)	1 John 5:14	(23)	John 14:27
(8)	Jeremiah 29:13	(24)	Psalm 1:1-3
(9)	Matthew 6:7-13	(25)	John 14:1
(10)	Matthew 18:19	(26)	Matthew 6:25-33
(11)	Isaiah 65:23-24	(27)	Psalm 23:1-6
(12)	Matthew 6:6	(28)	Mark 12:30-31
(13)	Luke 11:9-10	(29)	Hebrews 12:1-2
(14)	Isaiah 58:9-11	(30)	John 4:14
(15)	Psalm 127:1	(31)	Matthew 5:13-16
(16)	Psalm 66:18		

5. Witness for God your experience to others.

This natural expression may happen in the prayer group, with friends, on the telephone or in the normal life of the church.

NOTE: **The great experiment** works best on a voluntary basis, not an imposed discipline. It can also be used as a voluntary part of the following integrated study on prayer.

Prayer

Week 1 **Powerful Prayer**
Scriptures: 1. 2 Chronicles 7:14
2. James 5:16
3. 1 John 3:22
4. John 15:6-7
5. Mark 11:24-25
6. Philippians 4:6
7. 1 John 5:14

Personal study (Try half an hour at the beginning of your day)
1. Read the scripture for the day. Pray and meditate on this scripture. Write out in less than 50 words how this scripture applies to your life.

2. Write out an act of kindness or generosity that you will do today for someone, unexpected by them. Keep a written record of (i) the reaction of the person to whom the kindness is extended, and (ii) the effect of this act upon you personally.

3. Write out carefully how you would like to build and develop your life. Take your time. One well prayed out and thought out sentence per day is good progress. Take about 10 minutes for each of these three activities.

Group study (Try a small group of 5-10 people)
1. Give examples of answered prayer, perhaps one example from each person. Some may want to say 'I pass' and just enjoy listening. That's fine. In all group activity allow people to remain silent if they so desire.

2. Read the 7 scripture passages noting the conditions for powerful praying. These conditions could be summarised in your note books.

3. What conditions do you find easiest and hardest to fulfil? Comment together, being sensitive to the struggles we all have.

4. Dream a little! What would you really like to be or do? Pray together about those dreams.

Family study (Try a family hour once a week)
1. What kind of praying do you like? Each person could comment, e.g. silent, listening to someone else pray, reading one (as in children's books), writing one, saying some together such as grace at meals, Bible ones like The Lord's Prayer, saying 'Thank you' prayers, talking about things then someone praying about them, conversational prayer.

2. Read Philippians 4:6 together. What are some things you can (i) be thankful about, and (ii) ask God for?

3. Pray together about these things. You could pray 'Thank you' prayers. Some of you may want to write a one sentence prayer. You could write a family prayer with each person adding a sentence.

4. Place a sheet of paper on the wall or fridge or by the phone with the heading 'Thank you God for'. Leave it there for anyone to write on during the week.

Church study (Try developing family worship on the week's theme)
1. Hymns and songs: these can be thanksgiving and prayer.

2. Prayer: expressions of thanks from the congregation.

3. Scripture: use passages from the week's studies.

4. Message: include illustrations of answered prayer, e.g. 2 Chronicles 7:11-14; examples from people in the congregation.

5. Response: Giving thanks in clusters.

Week 2 **Answered Prayer**
Scriptures: 8. Jeremiah 29:13
9. Matthew 6:7-13
10. Matthew 18:19
11. Isaiah 65:23-24
12. Matthew 6:6
13. Luke 11:9-10
14. Isaiah 58:9-11

Personal study
1. Read the scripture for the day. Pray about it and write out one sentence about how it applies to your life. It could be a sentence prayer or a resolution you want to make.

2. Write out an unselfish and unexpected act of kindness or generosity you will do today. Name the person, then act. Keep a note of the person's reaction and the effect of this act upon you personally.

3. Write down one of your life's goals each day and how you intend to fulfil that goal.

Group study
1. What circumstances or situations help you to pray best? Discuss and list these.

2. Read the scriptures for this week and find more of these circumstances or situations.

3. Plan ways of arranging such situations more often both individually and as a group.

4. Pray, using conversational prayer (anyone continues the conversation in prayer at any time). Seek God's guidance and help in fulfilling or adjusting these plans.

Family study
1. Pray together. This could be by reading a prayer from a child's book, one or two people praying if they

want to, saying 'Thank you'. If you had a 'Thank you God for' sheet, read it all. If you wrote prayers last week, you could read these again and see what has happened.

2. Read Matthew 6:7-13 and Luke 11:1-4. You could read The Lord's Prayer together in each one, and then pray the one used in your church.

3. What are some daily needs that God has given you — or given the ability to get them? Remember that each person is God's creation and gift to you all. You could pray, thanking God for those gifts.

4. Write on a sheet of paper some things you appreciate about each person in your family group. You could put this on the wall or fridge or by the phone and add to it during the week.

Church study

1. Hymns and songs: family favourites on a theme such as God's greatness and goodness.

2. Prayers: written by some families; litanies with adults and children.

3. Scripture: Matthew 6:7-15 or related themes.

4. Message: great prayers, e.g. The Lord's Prayer.

5. Response: clusters comment on prayer and action, e.g. Isaiah 58:9-11.

Week 3   Believing prayer
Scriptures: 15. Psalm 127:1
16. Psalm 66:18
17. Isaiah 59:1-3
18. Proverbs 28:9-10
19. Matthew 8:23-27
20. John 6:47
21. Ecclesiastes 3:1-8

Personal study

1. Read the scripture for the day and pray about what it means for you. Write a sentence applying that scripture to your life and attitudes.

2. Write out an unselfish and unexpected act of kindness or generosity you will do today. Name the person, then act. Record their reaction and its effect on you.

3. Write at least one sentence describing what you want to do with your life. Determine your priorities.

Group study

1. Recall a significant event in your life in the last month and tell why it was so meaningful to you.

2. Read the scripture passages, briefly sharing any response you have made to them during the week.

3. In the light of Ecclesiastes 3:1-8, indicate how you would really like to use your time personally, in your

family and in your church. How is faith needed? Can the group help?

4. Give symbolic gifts to each person in your group, perhaps relevant to their hopes and desires, e.g. a green light to move ahead, matches to light fires in people's lives.

Family study

1. What was one of the most interesting things to happen in each person's life during the week, or what did you like best this week?

2. Read Matthew 8:23-27 together. What do we learn about Jesus in that story? How can Jesus help us today? Note how he liked to be with his friends.

3. What do you like doing together? You could plan ways to do the things you like doing together more often, e.g. family picnic, visit friends, Saturday outing, play tennis. Perhaps you could put up a sheet this week where people can add ideas about things you would like to do together.

4. You could say or write prayers asking Jesus to help you in the tough times and good times.

Church study

1. Hymns and songs: focus on faith; expressions of trust in God.

2. Prayers: thanks for past blessing; trust in God for the future.

3. Scripture: possibly linking Ecclesiastes 3:1-8 with Matthew 8:23-27.

4. Message: God's care at all times; examples from the congregation.

5. Response: clusters recalling God's care and praying for future needs.

Week 4   Trusting prayer
Scriptures: 22. Psalm 55:22
23. John 14:27
24. Psalm 1:1-3
25. John 14:1
26. Matthew 6:25-33
27. Psalm 23:1-6
28. Mark 12:30-31
29. Hebrews 12:1-2
30. John 4:14
31. Matthew 5:13-16

Personal study

1. Read the scripture each day and pray about its meaning for you. Write out that meaning as it applies to your thoughts, words and actions.

2. Write out an unexpected, unselfish act you will do today, then do it. Note the person's reaction and its effect on you.

3. Write down how you really want to live your life. You could link this with thoughts from the daily scripture passage.

Group study

1. What has been significant in your prayer life lately? Discuss how this has happened.

2. Read the scripture passages, commenting on what they mean to you. You could comment by completing these sentences:
I need to . . .
I want to . . .

3. Write your name on a sheet of paper and pass it clockwise round the group. Each person writes comments of appreciation about your strengths. When finished everyone can reflect on the feedback they receive.

4. Pray for one another, trusting your way to God. Communion may be appropriate.

Family study

1. Read Psalm 23. Can anyone recite it, or sing it?

2. Jesus is the good shepherd (John 10:11). Read a story about this, or discuss it. What does it mean in your family?

3. How can you care for or help each other? You could put up a sheet with each person's name on it and room for others to write in things you can do for them this week.

4. How do you want God to help you? You could talk about this then pray about it too.

Church study

1. Hymns and songs: the Good Shepherd; God's care.

2. Prayer: thanks for God's care, from anyone.

3. Scripture: Psalm 23 and John 10:7-16.

4. Message: Families may contribute examples of God's loving concern for us.

5. Response: Clusters planning ideas for caring activities, e.g. church picnics or barbecues, visits to retirement villages or hospitals, church family nights, roller skating together, contacting people by phone or letter, and so on.

Relationship

Week 1	Love God and others
Scriptures:	1. Matthew 22:34-40
	2. Mark 12:28-34
	3. Luke 10:25-37
	4. Romans 13:8-10
	5. Galatians 5:13-15
	6. Galatians 6:1-2
	7. James 2:8

Personal study

1. Read the scripture for the day. Write out in a sentence or two how it applies to your life.

2. Note in a brief statement the kind of relationships you want in your life and ways you plan to build such relationships.

3. Write down one act of encouragement or personal help you will do for someone today. Later, note the response of the person you encouraged and its effect on you.

Personal study

1. Write notes on (i) what you really want to get from this group, and (ii) what you are willing to give to this group. Comment together.

2. Discuss specific goals for your group and then comment on ways of achieving them.

3. Read the scripture passages. Comment on priorities for your group from your goals.

4. Pray about your goals and plans to achieve them.

Family study

1. Can you think of something someone did for you? How did you feel about that?

2. Read Luke 10:25-37 dramatically.

3. Plan a play or role play that applies this passage to your situation.

4. Make a list of things you can do to help others in your family this week. Put it where you can see it during the week, and pray, asking God to help you do these things or think of more.

Church study

1. Use Luke 10:25-37 or similar passages.

2. Families and individuals could comment on ways people have helped them.

3. Make a list of things you can do as a church family to help others, e.g. visiting shut-ins, hospitals, old people's homes, mowing lawns, shopping for ill people, visiting friends and new people, church outings or activities such as picnics, barbecues, sport, writing letters, making phone calls.

Week 2   Love one another

Scriptures:
   8. John 13:34-35
   9. John 15:12, 17
  10. 1 Thessalonians 4:9
  11. 1 Peter 1:22
  12. 1 John 3:11, 23
  13. 1 John 4:7-12
  14. 2 John 5

Personal study

1. Meditate and pray about the scripture for the day. Write a sentence applying it to your life.

2. What goals do you have for your personal relationships? Each day write one specific goal for yourself, e.g. in your family, church, work, community.

3. Link your goal with something you will do for someone today. Note that.

Group study

1. Read the scripture passages without comment. Then reflect on their total impact for you. How do these verses affect you?

2. Find ways of applying these scriptures in your group, e.g. affirm strengths of people in the group.

3. Consider ways of loving others beyond the group either personally, or as a group action.

4. Pray about this, seeking God's leading and help.

Family study

1. What is one good thing you like about each person in your family, starting with the youngest?

2. How did Jesus show love for other people? Everyone could think of one story about that.

3. Make a new list for your family. This time each person could say what they would like others to do to help them, and write that on your list to put up during the week.

4. Pray about doing some of those things.

Church study

1. Use John 13:34-35 or similar passages.

2. Families and individuals could report on ways they have been able to show love to others.

3. A few people, or the congregation, could ask questions of one or two leaders in the church about anything, including ways they can help them.

Week 3   Support one another

Scriptures:
  15. Galatians 5:22-26
  16. Ephesians 4:1-3
  17. Ephesians 4:32
  18. Colossians 3:8-11
  19. Colossians 3:12-14
  20. Romans 14:19
  21. Romans 15:7

Personal study

1. Pray about the scripture reading and write down how it applies to your life.

2. How do you want to live your life in the light of today's passage? Write that.

3. Write down how you will support someone today. Note the results of your act.

Group study

1. Read Galatians 5:22-26. Then individually list the names of everyone in your group, including your own. Beside each name write the most obvious fruit of the Spirit you see in them. You can use words from Galatians or other terms. Share these.

2. Read the scripture passages. Note the instructions for right relationships. Which do you find hardest to fulfil?

3. Each person could write a major goal he or she has, and beside that write ideas on what to do about it. How can the group help?

4. Pray for one another about those issues.

Family study

1. Read Galatians 5:22-23 and write down beside each person's name the fruit of the Spirit you see most in that person.

2. Can you think of any stories of Jesus which show the fruit of the Spirit in him?

3. You could draw a large tree with large fruit on it. Write the names of each person in one piece of fruit and some of the ways each one is like Jesus in their fruit. Put this up for the week, and add to it if you want to during the week.

4. Pray together for each person, asking Jesus to make each one more like him.

Church study

1. Use Galatians 5:22-26 or similar passages.

2. Families and individuals could suggest ways we can be more like Jesus.

3. Clusters or groups of a few families could talk about ways they can support one another.

Week 4   **Serve one another**

Scriptures: 22. John 13:12-17
               23. 1 Peter 5:5
               24. Hebrews 3:12-14
               25. Hebrews 10:24-25
               26. Esphesians 5:21
               27. Romans 12:9-13
               28. Romans 12:14-21

Personal study

1. Meditate on the scripture and write out its application to yourself.

2. Write down a relationship goal for yourself each day.

3. Plan how to serve someone today and note the results for them and you.

Group study

1. Review the month's studies. What have you learned? In what ways have you grown?

2. Read the scriptures and comment on how they apply to your relationships and growth.

3. Give symbolic gifts to each person in your group as one response, e.g. a green light for someone needing courage, a postage stamp for someone needing to contact friends.

4. Conclude with appropriate mutual service. Foot washing may suit your group. You could pray for each person in turn. Communion may be appropriate.

Family study

1. Read or tell the story of John 13:1-17

2. Talk about how you can obey Jesus' command in your family.

3. Draw a family shield or crest with the words LOVE ONE ANOTHER at the top or bottom of it. Divide it into sections, one for each person in your family. In each section draw one person doing something for others. Put it up for a week and add comments to it if you want to.

4. Pray together asking God to help you serve one another.

Church study

1. Use John 13:1-17 or similar passages.

2. Families and individuals could comment on ways church life can help us serve one another.

3. Clusters could comment on the strengths or qualities they see in each peson in their cluster and pray, thanking God for those strengths and asking for help in using them in service for others.

Good news

Week 1   **Jesus frees**

Scriptures: 1. Mark 1:1
               2. Mark 1:14-15
               3. Luke 4:16-20
               4. Matthew 4:23-25
               5. Matthew 11:4-6
               6. Luke 9:1-6
               7. Mark 16:15

Personal study

1. Note some aspect of the good news which applies to you today from the scripture reading.

2. Apply this to your relationships with others today. What can you say or do?

Group study

1. Recall a time when someone helped you know the freedom Jesus brings. How did that happen?

2. Read the scripture passages and comment on the overall picture of the gospel there.

3. How can we help people know freedom? Plan some specific ways as a group or as individuals.

4. Pray about those plans.

Family study

1. What is a favourite Bible verse or song for you? You could recite, read or sing it.

2. Tell or read the story in Luke 4:16-30.

3. Why do you think Jesus read that and why do you think the people were upset?

4. What are some things you think Jesus would do in your home? Choose different ways to answer that: draw a picture, write a poem, make a play, discuss the topic, do some of the things Jesus would do, pray about it.

Church study

1. Link scriptures you use with songs, hymns, and prayers.

2. Families or individuals could prepare prayers, poems, songs, skits or testimonies illustrating the theme.

3. Clusters could consider ways to bring freedom or help to others and pray for others.

Week 2   **Jesus delivers**

Scriptures:
8. Acts 15:7-11
9. Acts 20:24
10. Romans 1:15-17
11. Ephesians 1:13-14
12. Colossians 1:11-14
13. 2 Corinthians 4:3-6
14. 2 Corinthians 5:17-21

Personal study

1. Note some aspect of the good news which applies to you today from the scripture reading.

2. Apply this to your relationship with others today. What can you say or do?

Group study

1. What does being a new creation mean for you? Note 2 Corinthians 5:17-21.

2. As you read these scripture passages note the things from which you have been delivered.

3. How can we know fuller deliverance and bring this to others?

4. Pray about those ideas.

Family study

1. Who have been some of your best friends? How did that happen?

2. Read or tell a story about Jesus making us friends of God, as in 2 Corinthians 5:17-21.

3. Try memorising 2 Corinthians 5:17.

4. Show what being friends with God is like, using different activities such as singing, dancing, acting a story, drawing, talking about it, praying about it.

Church study

1. Express passages like Romans 1:16 or 2 Corinthians 5:17 in songs and prayers.

2. Families or individuals could present activities on the theme or give testimonies.

3. Clusters could look at possibilities for reaching out to others in the church and community and pray about that.

Week 3   **Jesus saves**

Scriptures:
15. John 1:1-5
16. John 1:14-18
17. John 1:29-34
18. John 3:14-17
19. John 10:7-11
20. John 11:25-26
21. John 20:30-31

Personal study

1. Note some aspect of the good news which applies to you today from the scripture reading.

2. Apply this to your relationship with others today. What can you say or do?

Group study

1. What are some of your favourite Bible verses or passages? How did they become significant to you?

2. Which of the statements in the readings are particularly meaningful to you just now? Why?

3. How can we help others understand the gospel? List ways.

4. Pray about those ways.

Family study

1. What is some good news that happened this week?

2. Read, recite or tell about John 3:14-17

3. How does John 3:16 help us understand the best good news?

4. Find creative ways to express that in talk, writing, picture, action, prayer. An example:

God loved the world so much he gave his

Only begotten

Son so that whoever believes in him will not

Perish but have

Everlasting

Life.

Church study

1. Celebrate John 3:16 or some other passage in song and prayer.

2. Families or individuals could present creative expressions of John 3:16 prepared during the week, including testimonies.

3. Clusters could think of ways to bring good news to others, including visits to old people's or children's homes to do things you did in church.

Week 4   Jesus reigns
Scriptures: 22. Romans 10:9-13
               23. 1 Corinthians 15:1-4
               24. Philippians 2:5-11
               25. 2 Timothy 2:8-10
               26. Hebrews 1:1-3
               27. Hebrews 12:1-2
               28. Revelation 5:9-14

Personal study

1. Note some aspect of the good news which applies to you today from the scripture reading.

2. Apply this to your relationship with others today. What can you say or do?

Group study

1. What grabs you most about the Easter story?

2. Read the scriptures then comment on what the risen Lord means for you?

3. What would you like the risen Lord to do for you or through you?

4. Pray about those desires. Sharing communion may be appropriate.

Family study

1. What songs do you know about Jesus' death and resurrection?

2. Read the song in Philippians 2:5-11.

3. What does the creed 'Jesus Christ is Lord' mean for yourself and your family?

4. Work out some creative ways to express that creed, e.g. write the passage in your own words, make your own song, write a poem, draw a picture or symbol, make a banner.

Church study

1. Sing and celebrate on a theme such as Philippians 2:5-11.

2. Families or individuals could express the theme in words, actions, prayer or testimony.

3. Clusters could think of ways to celebrate and involve others such as a breakfast barbecue.

The Church

Week 1   Christian community
Scriptures: 1. Matthew 16:13-20
               2. Matthew 18:15-20
               3. Acts 2:41-47
               4. Acts 11:25-26
               5. Acts 13:1-3
               6. Acts 14:23-27
               7. Acts 15:1-4

Personal study

1. Write down the application of the scripture for you today.

2. Note how you can live in Christian community today:
   a. in your own home and work;
   b. in relationship with others.

Group study

1. What were one or two of your most significant experiences in the Christian community, the church?

2. What are the most important insights from the scripture readings for you?

3. How would you most like to share in the life of the church, and how can the group help you?

4. Pray together about these desires.

Family study

1. What does each of you like most about the church? Note friends, activities, singing, helping, learning, and so on.

2. Read or tell about the early church from Acts 2:41-47. What would you like most in that kind of church?

3. Can you plan anything you would like to do that those Christians did? Note, inviting a family or friends to your place for tea or supper, lending books, having a pot-luck tea — everyone brings something.

4. Pray about your plans.

Church study

1. Consider Acts 2:41-47 or similar passages.

2. Discuss in groups and report: What are significant things your church is doing:
   a. for its Christian community;
   b. for the general community?

3. Express your response in prayers or songs or words of thanksgiving and intercession.

Week 2   **Powerful community**
Scriptures:
8. Acts 1:1-8
9. Acts 2:1-4
10. Acts 4:29-33
11. Ephesians 1:15-23
12. Ephesians 3:20-21
13. Ephesians 5:18-33
14. Colossians 1:15-20

Personal study

1. Write down the application of the scripture for you today.

2. Note how you can live in powerful community today:
   a. in your own home and work;
   b. in relationship with others.

Group study

1. In what ways have you discovered God's power in your life and in church life?

2. What picture of the church do you see most clearly in the scripture readings?

3. How can you help the church become more like that picture?

4. Pray about that for one another.

Family study

1. What are some good things you know about people in your church?

2. Summarise the story of Peter and John in Acts 3 and 4. A Bible story book may help, or you could read Acts 3:1-10; 4:1-4, 23-24a, 31.

3. What are some good things you or your family could do for others in the church. Plan some.

4. Pray about your plans.

Church study

1. Consider Acts 1:1-8 or similar passages.

2. Share testimonies: What has God done in your life recently?

3. Express your response in prayers or songs or words of praise and worship.

Week 3   **Spirit-filled community**
Scriptures:
15. John 20:1-22
16. Acts 1:5, 8; 2:1-4
17. Acts 4:31; 6:1-4
18. Acts 8:14-16
19. Acts 9:17-19
20. Acts 10:44-48; 11:15-17
21. Acts 19:1-7

Personal study

1. Write down the application of the scripture for you today.

2. Note how you can live in Spirit-filled community today:
   a. in your own home and work;
   b. in relationship with others.

Group study

1. What is your picture of a Spirit-filled community?

2. What picture do you have of the early church from the scripture readings?

3. What has been your experience of the Spirit and what more do you expect?

4. Pray together about those expectations.

Family study

1. Think of some people you know who have the Spirit of Jesus. What are they like? e.g. loving, caring, helpful.

2. Remember or read the story of the Ascension and Pentecost, Acts 1:6-11; 2:1-4.

3. How can you or your family show the Spirit of Jesus to others? Plan ways to do that.

4. Pray about your plans.

Church study

1. Consider Acts 2:14 or similar passages.

2. Discuss in clusters: What does it mean to be a Spirit-filled community?

3. Pray in clusters about being that kind of community.

Week 4   **Gifted community**
Scriptures: 22. 1 Peter 4:7-11
            23. Romans 12:3-8
            24. Ephesians 4:7-16
            25. 1 Timothy 3:1-13
            26. 1 Corinthians 12:1-11
            27. 1 Corinthians 12:27-31
            28. 1 Corinthians 13:1-13

Personal study

1. Write down the application of the scripture for you today.

2. Note how you can live in gifted community today:
   a. in your own home and work;
   b. in relationship with others.
(The *Gifts check list* on page 28 may help you.)

Group study

1. What do you see as some of your spiritual gifts? You could use the *Gifts check list* on page 28.

2. How do you see your gifts functioning in the church? Note the wide range in the scripture readings.

3. You could pass a sheet of paper round the group with your name on it so everyone can write comments about the gifts or strengths they see in you, or do that verbally for each person in turn.

4. Pray together about using your gifts for God's glory. Communion maybe appropriate.

Family study

1. What are gifts or abilities you see in each person in your family?

2. Describe or read the picture of the church as a body in 1 Corinthians 12:14-19.

3. Draw a large outline of a body on paper and write on it ways your family can help or serve others. Then plan to do some of those things.

4. Pray about your plans.

Church study

1. Consider 1 Corinthians 12:12-26 or similar passages.

2. Comment in groups on the gifts you see in different people in your group or how they have helped you.

3. Pray for one another in those groups.

Mission

Week 1   **The great example**
Scriptures: 1. Matthew 1:18-25
            2. Luke 4:16-21
            3. Luke 7:18-23
            4. Mark 10:42-45
            5. Luke 22:24-26
            6. John 13:12-17
            7. Philippians 2:5-11

Personal study

1. Read the scripture and note its application to you.

2. Write down how you will apply it today.

Group study

1. What impresses you most about Jesus' life?

2. What picture of mission does Jesus give us in these readings?

3. How can you apply that to your life now and the group now? Be specific.

4. Pray about that.

Family study

1. How did someone in your family serve you this week?

2. Read or tell John 13:1-17

3. Plan ways to wash feet this week, or something like that, for people in your family. You could note what you will do for each person each day.

4. Ask Jesus to give you ideas and help you.

Church Study

1. Sing or read servant songs and prayers.

2. Ask for insights on Philippians 2:5-11 or a similar passage.

3. Groups could prepare a brief presentation on the theme, either beforehand or on the spot.

Week 2   **The great command**
Scriptures: 8. Matthew 22:34-40
            9. Mark 12:28-34
            10. Luke 10:25-37
            11. John 13:34-35
            12. James 2:8
            13. 1 John 4:7-21
            14. 1 Corinthians 13:4-8a, 13

Personal study

1. Read the scripture and note its application to you.

2. Write down how you will apply it today.

Group study

1. Recall some times when you discovered God's love in new ways through other people.

2. Glance over the readings and comment on which verse or verses have special meaning for you.

3. What are some ways in which you best express your love (a) for God, and (b) for others?

4. Pray about that.

Family study

1. How have people shown you love lately?

2. Read or tell the story of the Good Samaritan in Luke 10:30-37.

3. How can you go and do the same this week (a) in your family, (b) with your friends. You could list some ideas, or draw them, or do some now.

4. Ask Jesus to give you ideas and help you.

Church study

1. Sing or read love songs and prayers.

2. Ask for examples of 1 Corinthians 13:4-7.

3. Groups could consider how to show love in the church and for others.

Week 3   The great commission

Scriptures:
1. Matthew 28:16-20
2. Mark 16:15-20
3. Luke 9:1-6
4. Luke 10:1-9
5. Luke 24:45-49
6. John 20:21-23
7. Acts 1:6-8.

Personal study

1. Read the scripture and note its application to you.

2. Write down how you will apply it today.

Group study

1. Comment on turning points in your life when you moved in new directions.

2. Which commissioning statement in the readings has most meaning for you?

3. What do these commissioning statements mean for you at this stage in your life?

4. Pray about that.

Family study

1. How has someone helped you last week?

2. Read or tell the Matthew 28:16-20 story.

3. What are some things Jesus has told you to do? Make a list or draw or act some of those things.

4. Ask Jesus to give you ideas and help you.

Church study

1. Sing or read discipleship songs and prayers.

2. Ask for testimonies of how people became disciples of Jesus when someone lived out Matthew 28:18-20.

3. Groups could think of ways to encourage mission through friendship.

Week 4   The great compulsion

Scriptures:
22. John 1:29-34
23. John 7:37-39
24. John 14:12-16
25. John 20:21-22
26. Acts 1:1-9
27. Acts 2:1-4, 41-47
28. Ephesians 5:18-20.

Personal study

1. Read the scripture and note its application to you.

2. Write down how you will apply it today.

Group study

1. What has been your experience of the Spirit lately?

2. Read the scriptures and comment on their meaning for the mission of the church.

3. What would you like the Spirit of Jesus to do in or through you?

4. Pray about that. Communion may be appropriate.

Family study

1. How did you help someone last week?

2. Read or tell about life in the early church as in Acts 2:41-47.

3. How can you help other families or single people? Think of ideas and begin to make a list.

4. Ask Jesus to give you ideas and help you.

Church study

1. Sing or read Spirit songs and prayers.

2. Ask for stories of how Acts 1:8 came true in people's lives.

3. Groups could pray for one another about living in the power of the Spirit as Jesus' witnesses.

Finding new life

Week 1 **God's love**
Scriptures:
1. Jeremiah 31:3
2. Jeremiah 31:33:34
3. Ezekiel 34:14-16
4. John 3:16
5. Isaiah 55:1-3
6. Jeremiah 29:11-13
7. Psalm 145:18

Personal study

1. Meditate: apply the daily reading to your life in a summary statement.

2. Act: apply the reading to your attitude toward others today.

Group study

1. When have you been most aware of God's love?

2. Read the scriptures and comment on the overall picture of God they give.

3. How can you share God's love more fully with others? Make a list.

4. Pray for help in responding more fully to God's love and reaching out to others with it.

Family study

1. How do we know God loves us?

2. Read or recite John 3:16.

3. Express this in some creative way: picture, song, play, record or cassette.

4. Say thanks in your own way for God's love and find ways to share that love with others this week such as visiting someone, inviting a lonely person for a meal or supper, writing a letter, making a phone call.

Church study

1. Celebrate God's love in worship.

2. Comments: How has God's love changed your life?

3. Pairs or clusters: talk or pray about responding to God's love and grace.

Week 2 **Salvation**
Scriptures:
8. Micah 4:1-6
9. Isaiah 55:9
10. Ephesians 6:19
11. John 11:21-27
12. Romans 5:6-8
13. Isaiah 53:4-6
14. Colossians 1:13-14

Personal study

1. Meditate: apply the daily readings to your life in a summary statement.

2. Act: apply the reading to your attitude towards others today.

Group study

1. How did you first become involved in the church and what does it mean for you now?

2. Which statement in the readings grabs you most and why?

3. What does salvation mean to you?

4. Pray for deeper awareness of 'a full and free salvation through faith in Jesus' name'.

Family study

1. Who loves you even when you are wrong or bad?

2. Read or tell about Romans 5:6-8.

3. Can you think of anyone who died for others? How was Jesus' death different from that?

4. Give thanks for God's love and see if you can go out of your way to show love to someone else this week.

Church study

1. Celebrate salvation in worship.

2. Comments: What does salvation mean for you?

3. Pairs or clusters: talk or pray about salvation.

Week 3   Abudant life
Scriptures: 15. Ezekiel 36:22-28
            16. John 14:14-18
            17. Acts 2:1-4
            18. Acts 19:5-7
            19. Galatians 5:22-23
            20. 1 Corinthians 12:4-11
            21. Ephesians 2:19-22

Personal study

1. Meditate: apply the daily reading to your life in a summary statement.

2. Act: apply the reading to your attitude toward others today.

Group study

1. What puzzles or interests you most about being filled with the Spirit of God?

2. What activity of the Spirit in the readings do you desire most?

3. What do you sense God wants to do in your life?

4. Pray for one another about your desires and response to the Lord.

Family study

1. If Jesus came to your home for a week what do you think would happen?

2. Read or explain Galatians 5:22-23.

3. Write each person's name and beside each one write or draw some of the fruit of the Spirit you see in that person.

4. Thank God for the Spirit in your lives and think of ways to share the fruit of the Spirit with others.

Church study

1. Celebrate abundant life in worship.

2. Comments: What qualities of Spirit-filled life impress you?

3. Pairs or clusters: talk or pray about the qualities or fruit of the Spirit you see in each other.

Week 4   Receiving God's gift
Scriptures: 22. Titus 3:4-6
            23. John 7:37-38
            24. Mark 1:15
            25. Acts 2:38-39
            26. 1 Corinthians 6:9-10
            27. Romans 4:20-21
            28. Luke 11:9-13

Personal study

1. Meditate: apply the daily reading to your life in a summary statement.

2. Act: apply the reading to your attitude toward others today.

Group study

1. What, for you, is the most meaningful or profound aspect of God's gift of the Holy spirit?

2. What do the readings emphasise for you about repentance?

3. What specific need would you like others to pray with you about?

4. Pray about those needs or desires. Communion may be appropriate.

Family study

1. When have you decided to do something good or new, and done it?

2. Read or describe Mark 1:14-15.

3. What good or new things can you decide to do?

4. Pray about those new things and give thanks for the ways God helps you.

Church study

1. Celebrate God's goodness in worship.

2. Comments: What gifts from God have blessed you?

3. Pairs or clusters: talk or pray about the gift of God's Spirit in your lives and what this means for others.

Living new life

Week 1   **Life in the Spirit**

Scriptures:
1. 1 Peter 5:7-9
2. Matthew 5:23
3. Ephesians 6:18
4. Romans 8:6
5. 1 Corinthians 14:1
6. 1 Corinthians 3:1-3
7. 2 Corinthians 4:16; 5:1, 5

Personal study
1. Meditate: apply the daily reading to your life in a summary statement.

2. Act: apply the reading to your attitude toward others today.

Group study
1. What are some of your main aims in life?

2. What do the readings suggest about goals in life?

3. How can you combine making love your aim with living in the Spirit's power?

4. Pray for that.

Family study
1. What are some of your favourite mottos?

2. What would a motto MAKE LOVE YOUR AIM mean for you? (See 1 Corinthians 14:1.)

3. Write or draw or create a motto that puts that into practice, such as 'a tidy room makes a happy home'.

4. Ask Jesus to help you live your motto.

Church study
1. Celebrate life in the Spirit in worship.

2. Comments: examples of living in the Spirit.

3. Pairs or clusters: talk or pray about living in the power of the Spirit.

Week 2   **Growth**

Scriptures:
8. John 4:14
9. John 15:5-6
10. Ephesians 4:22-23
11. Luke 5:15-16
12. 2 Timothy 3:15-17
13. Acts 2:41-47
14. Colossians 4:5-6

Personal study
1. Meditate: apply the daily reading to your life in a summary statement.

2. Act: apply the reading to your attitude toward others today.

Group study
1. What growth do you see in your life? Others could add their observations also.

2. What aspects of Christian living and growth speak strongly to you from the readings?

3. How can you grow stronger in these areas?

4. Pray for that.

Family study
1. What do you like best about Jesus?

2. How is Jesus' life shown in us? (See John 15:5-6.)

3. Draw a vine with a wide trunk and large leaves and grapes. Write qualities of Jesus' life in the trunk and qualities of his life you see in each person on one or more of the leaves or bunches of grapes.

4. Ask Jesus to help you grow in these qualities.

Church study
1. Celebrate growth in worship.

2. Comments: examples of growth.

3. Pairs or clusters: talk or pray about growth in your lives.

Week 3   Transformation in Christ

Scriptures: 15. Philippians 2:13
              16. Philippians 3:8-9
              17. James 1:2-4
              18. 1 Corinthians 10:13
              19. Romans 8:28
              20. Romans 12:4-5
              21. Hebrews 10:24-25

Personal study

1. Meditate: apply the daily reading to your life in a summary statement.

2. Act: apply the reading to your attitude toward others today.

Group study

1. Relax in prayer thanking God for specific blessings.

2. What aspects of transformation in Christ do the readings highlight for you?

3. Put Hebrews 10:24-25 into practice in some way. An example: describe an imaginary home for each person — big windows for those with vision, filing cabinet for well organised people, large fridge for someone keen on hospitality, and so on.

4. Pray about that.

Family study

1. What physical things do you like doing?

2. If your family is like a body, what parts of it can you be? e.g. hands tidying your room, setting the table; arms nursing the baby; feet going shopping (see Romans 12:4-5).

3. Draw a large body outline and write your name with things you can do or like doing on different parts of the body. Examples: on head — listening, singing, watching family members play sport; on hands — cooking, making things, ironing; on legs — walking the dog, playing sport, and so on.

4. Ask Jesus to help you do these well.

Church study

1. Celebrate transformation in Christ in worship.

2. Comments: examples of transformation.

3. Pairs or clusters: talk or pray about transformation in Christ in your lives.

Week 4   Led by the Spirit

Scriptures:
This week allow the Holy Spirit to guide you to scriptures you need in some way for your life.

Personal study

1. Meditate: apply the daily reading to your life in a summary statement.

2. Act: apply the reading to your attitude toward others today.

Group study

1. Meditate in silence for 3 to 5 minutes and write down what the Spirit of God is saying to you about your own growth or life in the group.

2. Share these impressions with the group and illustrate them from scripture or let others add their insights.

3. What has emerged as a need or direction for your group?

4. Pray for that. Communion may be appropriate.

Family study

1. Who are some of your favourite characters in the Bible? Why?

2. Draw a picture or make a model or write something about one of your favourite characters.

3. Talk about ways each person is like their favourite characters.

4. Ask Jesus to help you as God helped them.

Church study

1. Celebrate the Spirit's presence in worship.

2. Comments: examples of being led by the Spirit.

3. Pairs or clusters: talk or pray about the Spirit's leading in your life and how this can bless others.

Faith alive

Week 1 **Faith alive in you**
Scriptures: 1. Habakkuk 2:4
2. Romans 1:17
3. Galatians 3:11
4. Hebrews 10:38
5. Hebrews 11:1, 6
6. Ephesians 2:8-9
7. John 14:1

Personal study

1. Meditate on the reading and note how it applies to you.

2. Plan something you will do for someone today.

Group study

1. What have been one or two major turning points in your faith journey?

2. In the light of the scripture readings what is your present faith challenge?

3. How can the group help you grow in faith?

4. Respond in prayer.

Family study

1. What would you like to achieve or do this year?

2. Read Hebrews 11:5-6 and Genesis 5:21-24 and talk about Enoch's faith and goals.

3. Can you list some family goals?

4. Pray for help in reaching those goals.

Church study

1. Worship: express personal faith.

2. Invite or plan testimonies of finding faith or growing in faith.

3. Pray in faith for specific needs.

Week 2 **Faith alive in your lifestyle**
Scriptures   8. Genesis 1:26-31
9. Micah 6:8
10. Isaiah 58:6-12
11. Matthew 6:24-34
12. Matthew 23:23-24
13. Matthew 25:31-46
14. James 2:14-26

Personal study

1. Meditate on the reading and note how it applies to you.

2. Plan something you will do for someone today.

Group study

1. What impresses you about people who have made a difference for good in people's lives?

2. How can the scripture readings help you to make a difference in people's lives?

3. What is the near edge of some great needs that you can do something about (a) personally, and (b) as a group?

4. Pray in faith that leads to action.

Family study

1. Read or tell the parable in Matthew 25:31-46.

2. What kind of needs do you know about (a) in your family, and (b) in others?

3. Can you plan any ways of helping those people? Some examples: mum's day off; help dad with jobs; help each other tidy rooms; visit sick people; take shut-ins for a drive; take a hot meal to someone elderly or very busy; invite a lonely person to your place; write a letter or make a phone call; and so on.

4. Pray for help in helping others.

Church study

1. Worship: express faith through service.

2. Invite or plan testimonies of putting faith into action.

3. Pray in clusters for specific needs and plan ways to help.

Week 3 **Faith alive in your church**
Scriptures: 15. Deuteronomy 11:18-21
16. Joel 2:28-32
17. Luke 2:41-52
18. Matthew 18:1-5
19. John 13:1-17
20. Acts 2:43-47
21. Acts 4:32-37

Personal study
1. Meditate on the reading and note how it applies to you.

2. Plan something you will do for someone today.

Group study
1. Dreams and visions: imagine your ideal church.

2. Plans and prayers: how could your group put some of those dreams into practice?

3. Make a list: write ideas and specific action steps you can take.

4. Pray about these plans as you discuss them.

Family study
1. What are some things people in the church have done for you?

2. How did people help each other in the early church? Note Acts 4:32-37.

3. List some things you could do to help people in your church. Plan to do some of them.

4. Pray for help in doing those things.

Church study
1. Worship: express faith with vision.

2. Invite or plan testimonies of expressing faith in your church community.

3. Pray about growing together in faith.

Week 4 **Faith alive in your community**
Scriptures: 22. Genesis 12:1-3
23. Exodus 3:7-10
24. Ezekiel 3:16-21
25. Nehemiah 2:1-6
26. Jonah 3:1-5
27. Isaiah 61:1-3
28. Luke 4:18-21

Personal study
1. Meditate on the reading and note how it applies to you.

2. Plan something you will do for someone today.

Group study
1. What do you see as God's leading for your life?

2. What gifts or strengths do you have for your mission or calling? Others could add their ideas.

3. Give symbolic gifts to each person in the group to help them. Some examples: telescope to see the long view; coffee pot for hospitality; large lounge room for group meetings; a sail to catch the wind of the Spirit.

4. Pray specifically for each person. Communion may be appropriate.

Family study
1. What do you want to do when you grow up — or in the near future?

2. What things did Jesus do? Note Luke 4:16-21.

3. How would you like to help others in your work?

4. Pray for help in doing that.

Church study
1. Worship: express faith with compassion.

2. Invite or plan testimonies about serving the community in faith.

3. Pray for one another in your work in the community.

Great chapters — Old Testament

Week 1   The shepherd psalm
Scripture: Psalm 23

Personal study
1. Read the chapter each day, in different versions if possible, and note important truths for you. You could concentrate on a different verse each day.

2. Write down how these truths can affect your relationship with God and others today.

Group study
1. What is your favourite part of Psalm 23 or what has God revealed to you through the psalm?
Note: The shepherd (verses 1-4),
The banquet (verses 5-6).

2. When has this psalm had special meaning in your life?

3. How have you been able to help or encourage others with this psalm?

4. Pray together with gratitude and worship.

Family study
1. What did you like best at times when someone cared for you or looked after you?

2. Read or recite Psalm 23.

3. How does the Lord care for us? Express that in song, poetry, drawing, painting, action or story telling.

4. Give thanks for the Lord's loving care.

Church study
1. Celebrate the Lord's loving care.

2. People could give examples of how Psalm 23 has helped them.

3. Families or groups could express the psalm in different ways.

Week 2   Isaiah's vision
Scripture: Isaiah 6

Personal study
1. Read the chapter each day, in different versions if possible, and note important truths for you. You could concentrate on a different verse each day.

2. Write down how these truths can affect your relationship with God and others today.

Group study
1. What inspires or challenges you most about Isaiah 6?
Note: The vision (verses 1-7),
The call (verses 8-13).

2. When has this chapter had special meaning in your life?

3. Why do you think we sometimes resist God's will?
Note Matthew 13:14-15 and Acts 28:26-27.

4. Pray for openness to God's will and glory.

Family study
1. When have you remembered that God is with you?

2. Read or tell Isaiah 6: 1-8.

3. Listen to a record or find some creative way to think about God's greatness and glory.

4. Give thanks for God's great glory.

Church study
1. Celebrate God's glory.

2. People could give examples of how Isaiah 6 has challenged them.

3. Families or groups could express the message of the chapter in different ways.

Week 3   God's greatness
Scripture: Isaiah 40

Personal study
1. Read the chapter each day, in different versions if possible, and note important truths for you. You could concentrate on a different section each day.

2. Write down how these truths can affect your relationship with God and others today.

Group study
1. What inspires or challenges you most about Isaiah 40?
Note: Words of hope (verses 1-11),
         The incomparable God (verses 12-31).

2. When has this chapter, or parts of it, had special meaning in your life?

3. What does Isaiah 40:31 mean for you?

4. Pray together trusting in the Lord for help.

Family study
1. How big is God?

2. Read or tell about Isaiah 40:1-5, 8, 11, 28-31.

3. Listen to parts of Handel's *Messiah* or other music, or make your own, to consider God's greatness and glory.

4. Give thanks for God's power and help.

Church study
1. Celebrate God's greatness.

2. People could give examples of how Isaiah 40 has helped them.

3. Families or groups could express aspects of the chapter in different ways.

Week 4   The suffering servant
Scripture: Isaiah 53

Personal study
1. Read the chapter each day, in different versions if possible, and note important truths for you. You could concentrate on a different section each day.

2. Write down how these truths can affect your relationship with God and others today.

Group study
1. What inspires or convicts you most about Isaiah 53?
Note: The servant as seen by people (verses 1-3),
         The servant as seen by God (verses 4-6),
         The death as seen by people (verses 7-9),
         The death as seen by God (verses 10-12),

2. When has this chapter, or parts of it, had special meaning for you?

3. Note its application to Jesus in Matthew 8:16-17, Mark 15:28, Luke 22:37, Acts 8:32-35, and 1 Peter 2:21-25.

4. Pray together in gratitude. Communion may be appropriate.

Family study
1. Why is Jesus so special?

2. Read or tell the story of Acts 8:26-40 and Isaiah 53:7-8.

3. Think of some creative ways to express the amazing truth of Jesus' death and resurrection, such as song, writing, poetry, or drawing.

4. Give thanks for Jesus' death and resurrection.

Church study
1. Celebrate Jesus' death and resurrection.

2. People could give examples of how Isaiah 53 has had special meaning for them.

3. Families or groups could express aspects of the chapter in different ways, including sharing communion.

Great chapters — New Testament

Week 1   Faith
Scripture: Hebrews 11

Personal study
1. Read part of the chapter each day, in different versions if possible, and note important truths for you. You could concentrate on a different section each day.

2. Write down how these truths can affect your relationship with God and others today.

Group study
1. Which example of faith in Hebrews 11 impresses you most? Why?
Note Abel, Enoch, Noah, Abraham, Isaac, Jacob, Joseph, Moses' parents, Moses, Joshua, Gideon, Barak, Samson, Jephthah, David, Samuel and the prophets (Old Testament references can be found in footnotes as in the *Good New Bible*).What do verses 1 and 6 mean for you?

2. In what areas of your life would you like your faith increased? See Luke 17:5.

3. Pray in faith for one another.

Family study
1. How can we please God?

2. Choose a faith story like Hebrews 11:5 and Genesis 5:21-24 about Enoch to read or tell.

3. Why was that person a hero of faith? Can we be like that? Describe that faith in some way such as writing, poetry, drama, painting.

4. Ask God to help you grow in faith.

Church study
1. Celebrate faith in God.

2. People could give personal examples of faith in action.

3. Families or groups could illustrate Hebrews 11.

Week 2   Hope
Scripture: 1 Corinthians 15

Personal study
1. Read part of the chapter each day, in different versions if possible, and note important truths for you. You could concentrate on a different section each day.

2. Write down how these truths can affect your relationship with God and others today.

Group study
1. What inspires or challenges you most in 1 Corinthians 15?
Note: Christ's resurrection (verses 1-11),
        Our resurrection (verses 12-34),
        The resurrection body (verses 35-58).

2. Why is the resurrection vital for us? See verses 14 to 19.

3. In what ways would you like to know the power of the resurrection in your life? See Philippians 3:10-11.

4. Respond to these desires in prayer for one another.

Family study
1. Where is Jesus?

2. Read or tell the account of the resurrection in 1 Corinthians 15:3-9.

3. How do we know Jesus is with us? Show this in some creative way such as verse, song, drama.

4. Give thanks for the resurrection.

Church study
1. Celebrate our sure and certain hope.

2. People could give personal examples of our hope in life beyond death, such as near death experiences or the passing of Christians to glory.

3. Families or groups could illustrate 1 Corinthians 15.

Week 3 Love
Scripture: 1 Corinthians 13

Personal study

1. Read part of the chapter each day, in different versions if possible, and note important truths for you. You could concentrate on a different section each day.

2. Write down how these truths can affect your relationship with God and others today.

Group study

1. What inspires or challenges you most in 1 Corinthians 13?
Note: The priority of love (verses 1-3),
       The picture of love (verses 4-7),
       The permanence of love (verses 8-13).

2. Beside each person's name in your group write down the qualities of love you see in them.

3. How would you like to grow in love?

4. Pray for one another about these desires.

Family study

1. How do people show love in your family?

2. Describe love from 1 Corinthians 13:4-7.

3. Write the names of your family around a table top drawing, e.g. a rectangle. On the table top write the qualities of love you see in each person.

4. Thank God for your family in prayer or song.

Church study

1. Celebrate love for God and others.

2. People could give personal examples of love.

3. Families or groups could illustrate 1 Corinthians 13.

Week 4 God is love
Scripture: 1 John 4

Personal study

1. Read part of the chapter each day, in different versions if possible, and note important truths for you. You could concentrate on a different section each day.

2. Write down how these truths can affect your relationship with God and others today.

Group Study

1. What inspires or challenges you most about 1 John 4?
Note: True and false (verses 1-6),
       God is love (verses 7-21).

2. How have you come to know God's love more fully?

3. How would you like to know God's love more fully?

4. Pray about this for one another. Communion may be appropriate.

Family study

1. How did you find out about God's love?

2. Read and describe 1 John 4:8, 16.

3. Think of some ways to celebrate God's love, as in singing, listening to a record, writing verse, writing a letter, having a party.

4. Give thanks for God's love.

Church study

1. Celebrate God's love.

2. People could give personal examples of discovering God's love.

3. Families or groups could illustrate 1 John 4.

Jesus

Week 1   **Jesus' birth**

Scriptures:
1. Isaiah 7:14
2. Isaiah 9:6
3. Matthew 1:21
4. Matthew 1:23
5. Luke 1:31-33
6. Luke 2:11-14
7. Luke 2:21

Personal study

1. Meditate on these familiar verses each day and listen to the Lord.

2. Write down the Lord's word to you personally and its application to your relationships with others today.

Group study

1. What impresses you most about the birth of Jesus?

2. How does his birth affect your life, e.g. at Christmas, on Sundays, daily?

3. What does Emmanuel — God with us — mean for you right now?

4. Respond to that in prayer and worship.

Family study

1. What do you like best about Christmas?

2. What is Christmas about?

3. How much of the Christmas story can you remember? You could take turns telling parts of the story.

4. Celebrate Jesus' birth together. Some examples: singing carols, singing choruses about Jesus, reading some verses from the Bible, making a play, preparing for Christmas together, inviting people to a party, sending cards with greetings, writing letters.

Church study

1. Celebrate Jesus' birth.

2. Families or groups could present items.

3. People could tell about Christmas celebrations in the past or in different places and what was most meaningful to them.

Week 2   **Jesus' life**

Scriptures:
8. John 6:35, 48
9. John 8:12; 9:5
10. John 8:24, 28, 58
11. John 10:7, 9, 14
12. John 11:25
13. John 14:6
14. John 15:1, 5

Personal study

1. Meditate on these 'I AM' statements of Jesus and listen to his word to you.

2. Write down the Lord's word to you personally and its application to your relationships with others today.

Group study

1. What impresses you most about Jesus' life?

2. How does his life affect your life, e.g. his example, instructions, promises?

3. What do his unique claims such as his 'I AM' statements mean for you?

4. Respond to that in prayer and worship.

Family study

1. What do you like most about Jesus?

2. What are some of your favourite stories about Jesus? Why are they favourites?

3. What is something he said that you especially like? Why is that special to you?

4. Celebrate Jesus' life in some creative way. You can find ideas for all ages together in this book.

Church study

1. Celebrate Jesus' life.

2. Families or groups could present items.

3. People could tell how the story of Jesus first made an impression on them.

Week 3 — Jesus' Death

Scriptures:
15. Luke 23:34
16. Luke 23:43
17. John 19:27
18. Matthew 27:46; Mark 15:34
19. John 19:28
20. John 19:30
21. Luke 23:46

Personal study

1. Meditate on these words from the cross each day and listen to the Lord.

2. Write down the Lord's word to you personally and its application to your relationships with others today:

Group study

1. What impresses you most about Jesus' death?

2. How does his death affect your life? e.g. saviour, example, inspiration.

3. What do Jesus' words on the cross mean for you?

4. Respond to that in prayer and worship. Communion may be appropriate.

Family study

1. Why did Jesus come? Note Matthew 20:28 and 28:20.

2. What is God's best gift to you? Note John 3:16.

3. How can you thank God? Some ideas: believing, loving, obeying, praying, singing, serving, helping, following (being like Jesus).

4. Celebrate God's gift of Jesus together. Think of things you like to do together.

Church study

1. Celebrate Jesus' death.

2. Families or groups could present items.

3. People could tell what the cross means to them.

Week 4 — Jesus' resurrection

Scriptures:
22. John 1:1-4, 14
23. Ephesians 1:19-23
24. Philippians 2:5-11
25. Colossians 1:15-20
26. Hebrews 1:1-3
27. Revelation 1:4-8, 12-18
28. Revelation 4:8-11; 5:9-14

Personal study

1. Meditate on the scripture reading each day and listen to the Lord.

2. Write down the Lord's word to you personally and its application to your relationships with others today.

Group study

1. What impresses you most about Jesus' resurrection?

2. How does his resurrection affect your life? e.g. his authority, majesty, power, glory.

3. What do these scriptures about Jesus mean for you?

4. Respond to that in prayer and worship. A love feast or celebration may be appropriate.

Family study

1. Where is Jesus now?

2. What stories can you remember about Jesus' resurrection?
Note: Matthew 28, Mark 16, Luke 24, John 20-21, and Acts 1.

3. How does Jesus help us today?

4. Celebrate his resurrection by planning things you can do together now and in the future.

Church study

1. Celebrate Jesus' resurrection and glory.

2. Families or groups could present items.

3. People could tell what the Lord is doing for them now. Remember Matthew 28:20.

Resources

Available from **The Joint Board of Christian Education
Second Floor, 10 Queen Street
Melbourne 3000**
or your church bookstore.

For building relationships:

Keith Pearson, *R.A.P. Rapport and Personal
   Relationships*, JBCE

Keith Pearson, *Introduction to Group Dynamics*, JBCE

Bruce Turley, *Turning Points — An Invitation to Growth
   and Healing*, JBCE

Ross Kingham and Robin Pryor, *Out of Darkness — Out
   of Fire*, JBCE

For Bible study and prayer:

Kerygma: The Bible in Depth

Geoff Waugh, *Living in the Spirit*, JBCE

Geraldine Anderson (ed.), *40 Devotions that Work
   with Youth*, JBCE

Gordon Dicker, *The Bible with Understanding*, JBCE

Graham Millar, *Prayer Search*, JBCE

Hedley and Lyn Beare, *Praying in Secret*, JBCE

Joan Stott (ed.), *In God's Presence*, JBCE

For Program Planning:

Lance Armstrong, *Children in Worship*, JBCE

Leigh Pope (ed.), *8 Theme Studies for Camps and
   Other Settings*, JBCE

Geraldine Anderson (ed.), *50 Fun Programs That Work
   With Youth*, JBCE

Glen Smyth, *What Will We Do On Friday Night?*, JBCE

For all ages together:

Megan Coote (ed.), *Growing Together — How to Plan
   All-Ages Learning in the Church*, JBCE

Pat Baker and Mary-Ruth Marshall, *Simulation Games
   1, 2 and 3*, JBCE

Serendipity — Bible studies for youth and adults,
   JBCE/SU